The Girl With the Million Dollar Legs

The Girl With the Million Dollar Legs

by Porsche Lynn
and Brian Whitney

BearManor Media

2014

The Girl With the Million Dollar Legs

© 2014 Porsche Lynn and Brian Whitney

For information, address:

BearManor Media
P. O. Box 71426
Albany, GA 31708

bearmanormedia.com

Edited by Raymond R. Matthews

Typesetting and layout by John Teehan

Published in the USA by BearManor Media

ISBN—1-59393-593-5
978-1-59393-593-1

Introduction

When one gets to a certain point in their lives one often takes time to reflect on who they were, and who they have become. About a year ago I started to do that and while I did that I started to write. What you are about to read is a product of that reflection. If I were to sit down and tell my best friend a story about my life it would sound something quite like what you have in front of you right now.

I would say that while my life is a paradox, it is a paradox of all of the things that make me smile. I have a life that is full of many things that are somewhat contradictory. I do not see this as much of a problem as others sometimes do. I am 51 years old at the time of this writing and have come to a place of peace in my life. I have seen much hate, wrath and pure evil and somewhere along the way I did not choose to follow the path that was shown to me. I chose instead to follow a way of love, beauty, and benevolent compassion. I chose to heal my needy, wounded, abandoned little girl, heal my revengeful, manipulative adult and step onto a path with power, my path with heart. It took me many years over 20 to get to this place. I can honestly say that I am most content where I am. I truly have a wonderful life. I have always had a wonderful life even when it wasn't so pretty, I just wasn't awake enough to realize it.

This book will not be a book where I name all sorts of famous people I have slept with off set, nor will it be a book that focuses on my family or my childhood. If you did not know, when I was seven years old my Father shot my Mother in front of my grandmother and me. My Father later shot himself. This incident created a huge armoring on me in many ways, and while this incident will be mentioned in the book I focus more on my healing then I do on the pain that it caused me.

My life was forever changed. I was consumed with confusion, grief, anger and loss. Undeniably my life was sculpted by this action. However

1

I very rarely let it define who I was or make it my life. So while it most certainly is a part of who I am, you will find the topic mentioned only once. This book's focus is how all the different part of me came together to make for a most interesting journey expressed in three different times of my life, burlesque, porn and kink.

I guess the only warning that should accompany the reading of this book is that yes, it will use adult language, often very descriptive and lots of sarcastic humor. My editor warned me that sarcasm is not easily translated to the written page. With that said, I give you fair warning that you will be offered the choice to look at some of the situations of my life with the same open, anything goes, it's all out on the table humor that I do. Humor can crack even the most serious of moments, so that the river of emotion can flow through laughter. Thanks for reading my book. I hope you enjoy reading it as much as I did living it.

1

We always remember our firsts. Our first kiss, our first loves, and *the* first time. My first job in the adult entertainment industry was at the Cinema X in beautiful downtown Lansing, Michigan, where I procured a position as a peep show booth girl and as a burlesque entertainer.

It wasn't accidental that I wound up there nor was it a tragedy. Not even a little bit actually. That might make a better story perhaps but it wouldn't be true.

I had been offered the job quite at random. I had a boyfriend at the time; he drove me wild. I found him quite sexy and we used to bang like a porch door. We were always looking for new ways to turn each other on.

One night he took me to a drive-in theater, in Durand Michigan, commonly called the "Durand Dirties," that showed X-rated films. As we laid down in the back of my Dodge Omni, grinding against each other and watching people having sex on screen, a whole new world showed itself to me. I had never seen a porno before and couldn't believe what I was seeing; people were being so free, and engaging in sexual acts that I hadn't even thought of doing. I mean I didn't even know some of these things could be done! I was hooked, and completely mesmerized by what I saw on the screen. I was ridiculously turned on; so much so that I wasn't sure I should let my boyfriend know how much.

At one point I tore myself away from the screen long enough so that I could go to the concession booth to get a soda and use the bathroom. On the way I was approached by a very good looking older man. He introduced himself to me as Harry and asked if I was interested in joining the wet t-shirt contest that was happening at midnight. This confused me greatly as I honestly had no idea what he was talking about. The man explained to me that he picked several girls who would join him on the roof of the concession stand, wearing bikini bottoms and t-shirts. The t-shirts would then be wet with a hose, obviously clinging tight to my boobs and those of the other girls around me, leaving not much to the imagination. It is funny now to even think of it, but back then wet t-shirt competitions were all the rage. I think the prize was twenty dollars.

The thought of this form of exhibitionism appealed to me and turned me on. In reality, though, I wasn't sure I was ready for the public to see my body like that, much less compete in a contest. I told him this, but what I didn't tell him was how afraid I was of the whole thing. The man said he understood then added if I ever got seriously into doing a more private type of dancing he could give me a job if I was interested. It turned out Harry owned a theater in Lansing and was always looking for girls to work for him. He told me that he liked my look and invited me to come in sometime for an interview, then wrote down his number and gave it to me. I was assured that the work was legal, had flexible hours and I could earn good cash, although it did involve some nudity. It sounded exciting and I remember our conversation thinking to myself that I might actually do it and why not? I needed money, it sounded fun and might be a turn on.

I waited several weeks before following up on the offer. At the time I was in college. I was going to Michigan State and suddenly there was no more money. My college fund had run out and I needed a job that could help me through college and allow me some freedom as well.

So I called the number that I got from Harry and was told to come in the next day. And just like that I became a peep booth girl at Cinema X.

Cinema X was an enormous building with a large 150-seat theater that showed adult movies from about noon to midnight. It wasn't just movies though, there also was a store, which sold adult magazines, books, toys and novelties. About half of the building contained an area where live girls performed. There were nude shoeshine booths (doesn't that sound delightful? Be honest), and pool tables where girls played topless pool. The place was kind of like an amusement park for horny guys.

It also had a dance stage that had several small booths surrounding it. The customer entered the booth, and would place two quarters into a machine. When he did so a small window would come down, revealing the dance floor and a scantily clad girl gyrating to some kind of music. That girl would be me. How very nice to meet you.

Of course the thing was that two quarters would not buy a whole lot of time, three minutes to be exact. It was just a bit of a tease, you know. If the customer wanted to see more, either close up shots or nudity, he would have to put more quarters in the machine and dollar bills through the tip slot. Of course he would. So this began the "Kitty Hustle" between the customer and myself. Nobody sees the Kitty for free.

The dancer rewarded the tipping customer by removing more clothing and dancing closer to the window. Some guys would come in and just drop the two quarters and their window would only be open for a few minutes and then it was over. Others would just keep feeding bills through the slot. This would signify that the game was on.

There was a larger private booth in the back of the stage area where if I was doing my thing right and the customer was mesmerized, I would then hopefully seduce him into joining me in a one-on-one private masturbation show. These booths were more expensive. The private booths took nine quarters to activate the window. When the customer first walked in, the window appeared like a mirror, so all that he could see was himself when the quarters went in, the light would change and he could now see the girl just a few feet away. She still saw the window as a mirror. In other words, he was jacking off to what I was seeing too. This might seem a tad odd until one really thinks about what I would be looking at otherwise, and it also lets the customer be as freaky as he wanted to be. Of course some men would have been even more turned on if I could see what they were doing. Some men would have paid much more if I could see them doing their thing, but regardless that was the way it was set up. Later this system would be changed to a clear glass window, where the customer could see everything all of the time.

The nine quarters kept the window activated for the customer for about three minutes; if he wanted more time he had to place more quarters in. Almost all of them did of course. I mean, why would someone bother to spend a few dollars in quarters and then leave? Especially when the three minutes were usually just enough to get most guys worked up but not enough for them to get off.

There was also a tip slot next to the window, which is where the customer could place dollar bills. Obviously a guy who gave a twenty or more got the show that he wanted. The guy that gave a five would often be finishing up in the room with the window back down. The girl would communicate with the customer via phone, which allowed for a private conversation. So, basically a peep booth girl, doing her thing was pretty much a masturbation show between two people with lots of dirty talk. I thought this would have been difficult for me to do; that I would have been shy or uncomfortable, but I never was. It was funny how comfortable I felt.

At intermission of the movies the projectionist would have to change the rolls of film. This took about thirty minutes, and while this was going on the peep show booth girls would do a show on the stage of the theater. This was a burlesque show that involved costumes. Sometimes there would be a theme like a naughty nurse or bad teacher or some other traditional masturbation fantasy. We would usually dance four choreographed songs in the time that we had. We were usually on stage for a half an hour or so, which may not seem like a long time, but believe me it was.

The first song was a warm up: we would just be sexy and fun and dance around and smile a lot. The second song was a stripping song, in which I would remove my top and show my lovely boobs to everyone. The third song was a floorshow, and I mean that literally. I would put down a blanket on the floor and would roll around as much as possible removing my panties. The floorshow was pretty much a tradition everywhere I went over my career, and still is in most every strip club today. The fourth song was performed nude, usually with me jumping around and dancing as best I as could.

I really enjoyed the burlesque shows. I loved the creativity that we all employed, and what went into creating the shows; I loved wearing the costumes, the music and the whole spectacle of it. The crowd was usually pretty appreciative of my performances; after all, they were getting a free show and there wasn't anything else happening during intermission. I am certain that it was better than sitting in a dark theater or watching some silly cartoons in the middle of your porn. The main point of all this was to get the customers to come back to your booth and jack off for and to me when the movie was over. I always hoped to get the customers worked up and have them finish themselves off in my booth. This is where the real money was made, and it also became a point of pride. There was nothing worse than dancing your ass off on the stage for a half an hour and not getting any attention from the guys when you were done.

Once you got the customer to meet you back at your private viewing booth the point was to try and get some money. It was always much easier to get money from the guy when his pants were down and his dick was in his hands. I also got off on watching them jack off, plus the ego rush that they were jacking off to me was a huge bonus. I liked the power that I had, and I liked the control. I got really good at dancing, and playing with myself in the window, talking dirty on the phone and the whole hustle. I started working late, staying out even later and missing classes like crazy. I liked this life much better than my other one.

I had the opportunity to meet many famous porn stars that came to the theater on occasion to perform special shows for the crowd. I had the pleasure of meeting stars like Seka, Hyapatia Lee, Gail Palmer and Carol Connors, who was the star of *Candy Goes to Hollywood*. Meeting these women was always a bit intimidating but ultimately it was also revealing. First of all, they were all fairly nice and seemed like reasonably normal people. I thought they were going to be made of plastic or something, but no. That's when it hit me: these women were just like me. I could do what they were doing!

When I met these women I started to have my first thoughts of actually making porn movies. They were just people. Before this I was just dancing for fun. All of a sudden some seeds of thought entered my head that continued to germinate about me getting into the business for real.

It wasn't long before I dropped out of MSU, and I ended up getting my degree to be a LPN at a local community college. I did actually work in a hospital for about three months, which ended up being the very unpleasant bursting of my "I want to be a nurse " bubble. It was my first and perhaps last attempt at what is considered a normal life. I realized the staff was overworked, underpaid and it seemed to me that the doctors were obsessed with treating the symptoms of the sickness, illness or diseases and not actually finding the cause. They just seemed to keep writing prescriptions or doing surgeries, which seemed like a road to nowhere to me. If a patient was overweight, had high blood pressure, was diabetic, or whatever might be wrong with him or her, the doctors just kept writing the prescriptions and putting them in the hospital when things got bad to level them out with IV's, when really the patient would have been much healthier losing weight and being put on an exercise program.

My disillusion with the real world drove me deeper into Cinema X and further into the lifestyle that came with it. I also went to a local modeling school and tried to get as much legitimate modeling work as possible. My dream at the time was to become a runway model. I adored clothing and the runway and thought that I might have the look for it. I managed to get one meeting with the Ford Agency in New York City. My meeting lasted about fifteen minutes, with a very professional woman who informed me that there was no place for me in the modeling world. She said that I was too tall and gangly for print work and not tall enough or thin enough for the runway. I appreciated her honesty although it was devastating. She told me how she saw it with no bullshit. So I did return to Michigan and returned to the Cinema X, which was now my home away from home.

I made a commitment to really go for the burlesque thing; I wanted to travel with my show and I to be the best at it. It was what I was good at and it was what made me tick. I also loved the lifestyle. There was so much of it that called to me.

I had complete freedom to be who I wanted to be, could work when I wanted, play when I wanted, there was money to party with and lots of friends to share my good times. What more could I want out of life? My best friend at the time was a beautiful black woman who later became quite famous and was known as Angel Kelly. As a matter of fact when she went into the Legends of Erotica Hall of Fame, I did the induction ceremony. Who would have thought that two chicks from Lansing Michigan would both end up being members of the Adult Entertainment Industry Hall of Fame? We spent almost all of our time together over the years. We were together through thick and thin, through marriage and divorce, and highs and lows of all kinds. But back then we were just a couple of burlesque and peep show dancers that were out to rule the world.

She had come to work at Cinema X as well, and we soon forged a bond between us that was unbreakable. Have you ever had a partner in crime? I have been lucky enough to have a few. Kelly was my first and perhaps my best, although I did have quite a few more partners in crime over the years.

She and I started to travel to other cinemas of the same type in Michigan and then to other states like Indiana, Illinois, Ohio, and so on. We both perfected our skills in the business. We were becoming talented dancers and hustlers. We lived a life of constant partying with a little work thrown in here and there. We both loved to dance; we both loved music, clothes and sex. Our jobs were a perfect place for us to express and acquire all of these things. We looked like twins, one of us white, one black; we were both about the same height, around 5'9" with slender figures and faces. We felt unstoppable. We both drove a Datsun 280zx; mine was gold and hers was silver. We continued this lifestyle for about three years, until we hit a plateau. We both wanted more of everything: more money, more sex, more parties and we wanted something different. As exciting as our lives were they had become stale: it was the same faces and the same theaters.

It was time for a change and both of us knew it. We just didn't know how big the change was going to be.

2

At the time I was dating a man named Mike who owned several of the cinemas and who worked in the adult film industry. Mike was going to be moving out to Los Angeles and he had offered to assist both Angel and I get into the adult film biz. I never was quite sure what job he actually had in the porn business. I think in some way both of us liked it that way.

This was a decision that I did not take lightly. Even though I had lived a wild life over the past few years and had seen many things that many people would never see, I was still just twenty-three years old and was not hardened to the ways of the world just yet. I realized that working in porn would change my life forever. It was one thing to do what I was doing now. I could melt into normal life any time I wanted and no one would be the wiser. I knew that making fuck movies was something that needed some thought. It was the sort of thing that opened a door to some experiences but at the same time would close a door to other ones forever.

I took some time to think about all the aspects of being a porn star. How was I going to feel twenty years from now? Would I hate myself then? Could I really do it without hating myself? Would I get tired of sucking so much cock? Okay, I didn't really consider the last one.

I sat in the theater at Cinema X watching the films many times, thinking that I could do this, that I could be one of the women that I saw on the screen. To me it was really just a natural thing, having sex, not just a natural thing but a wonderful thing as well. The only difference between having sex in private and on the screen is that someone is filming it. I thought that I could drown the camera out and focus on the other person or persons that I was on camera with. I had a total crush on many of the leading men of porn back in the day, including John Leslie, Jaime Gillis and Paul Thomas. I loved watching the women too; they were all so sexy to me. Sharon Mitchell, Marilyn Chambers and Sharon Kane were just a few of the woman that I was drawn to. I looked at them as role models, as people I admired. They were strong, beautiful women and they were taking charge of their lives.

Before too long I realized that not only could I do it but that I wanted to do it. I packed up all my possessions, which at that time were mostly my clothes, in my 280zx and drove to LA. It was quite the different scene from Lansing. Back home there were only a few women with my looks and my willingness to be an adult entertainer. In L.A. they were everywhere. Mike and Angel made the move about three months before. Angel had already gotten her start in the film biz, and was starring in her first films. It was 1985. This was a big deal back then to have a black woman working in traditional porn movies. Angel was one of the first to do it, and she is still known for that to this day.

Most of the films were segregated, meaning, all the blacks were in movies together and whites were in movies together, I realize this sounds completely ludicrous today, but I swear this is how it was back then. I mean it was totally okay to have sex with three women at once or to bang them up the ass, but Heaven forbid a white man fuck a black woman. Or even worse what if a black man fucked a white woman? Yes, there were a few times when there were interracial movies, but they were pretty scandalous; for example in 'Behind the Green Door' there was some of that going on, but that movie was wild in general. There was one scene when someone came on Marilyn Chambers face and they showed a slow motion shot of the semen flying through the air for like seven minutes. No joke.

For whatever reasons the main stream producers were terrified of mixing blacks and whites in pornos. As I said, my friend Angel Kelly was one of the first black women to even appear in mainstream porno. It was so taboo back then.

It's important to remember that this was before the internet existed. This meant that porn was done for the masses and not for the people that were a certain kink. Whereas now, whether you are into hypnotized slaves, or women with big feet, you can find your type of porn within seconds. You could type "black man blows load on white woman's face" in a search engine and get thousands of hits right away. Back then, things were way more mainstream as far was what was shown on screen. Most of the porn that was being made was made for the average guy and if he was lucky, his girlfriend too.

Most of it was really of the traditional "oh the pizza guy just showed up at the party so now let's all fuck" kind of thing. Don't get me wrong, for the time it was incredibly scandalous, but like everything else the bottom line was that it was about money, anything too kinky could lead to an obscenity charge. And apparently a white dude banging a black chick was taking things way too far.

I had the incredible gift of having a boyfriend who knew the ins and outs of porn pretty well and he assisted me in making sure I got in front of all the right people. I like to think I would have made it without Mike, but who knows? So much of what happens in this business is who you know at first and then it's all up to you once you get your foot in the door.

I signed up with a talent agency called Reb's Pretty Girl International. I was willing to do anything and I first tried to get into every major men's magazine that I could. Once again, remember at this time, there was no internet and getting porn came in two ways: films that you could see in a theater that were shot on VHS, and of course there were magazines. Nowadays everyone is jacking off to the computer; back then that could not even be imagined. These were the days where husbands and sons hid their magazines in boxes under beds or buried them at the bottom of bureau drawers. If your wife or girlfriend found them, you could very well be in big trouble. Do people even buy magazines anymore?

One day I got the call to go to Flynt Publishing to apply for some magazine work. They published a lot of different magazines but their big one was called "*Hustler*". *Hustler* was the first magazine ever to publish "pink shots." I think you can guess what that means.

I was thrilled to be asked to meet with Mr. Flynt. First of all, you have to know that I had complete admiration and respect for Larry Flynt. I respected his tenacity to fight the system, legally and otherwise. He fought for the freedom for us to express ourselves sexually. He was and still is in my perception a great man, a warrior, and a champion for freedom and the rights of the individual. It was truly like meeting a hero of mine and I was very nervous.

I arrived at Flynt Publishing on Wilshire Blvd in Los Angeles, to see his offices took up an entire huge glass building. It was quite impressive really to see with my own eyes what one can build with money from making so-called smut. I entered the building wearing a chic red leather skirt, blouse and stiletto heels. I gained entrance to Larry Flynt's office, which was a large, immaculately decorated space. Larry was seated in his pimped-out gold wheelchair behind a large desk.

Mr. Flynt had been shot leaving a Georgia courtroom; he was in court because he was facing obscenity charges for sales of his magazines. They never officially caught the person who shot him, although a man named Joseph Paul Franklin confessed to the shooting while incarcerated for other crimes. Franklin said he did it because Flynt had published an interracial sexual photo in one of his magazines. The bullet that hit Larry hit his spinal column and left him paralyzed. I always wondered how this man managed to move on with his life with no pity. To me he was an incredible role model.

He welcomed me in the office and invited me to sit down; my legs were shaking, as were my hands when I shook hands with him. He made me feel very comfortable, and we did the usual getting to know you chit-chat. He asked me what magazines I wanted to be in, I said "I want to be in *Hustler* or *Chic*." Larry looked me in the eyes, after giving me a good look over, and said, "Well, you're much too classy to be in *Hustler*, How about if we shoot you for *Chic*? I will get my best photographer and makeup artist for you."

I was thrilled at the offer, but wondered what he saw in me that made him think I was too classy for *Hustler*? Would it prevent me from being a good cocksucker later on down the line? Shit, maybe I needed to work on slutting myself up for this whole porn thing. I left there feeling great about the job for *Chic* but wondering if I was going to be able to make it in porn. First I had been told that I was not cut out to be a runway model and then I'm told that I look too classy to lick sack in *Hustler*. What to do?

As I said before, much of the work that I got at first was because I had the incredible opportunity to have Mike, my boyfriend at the time, supporting me through this process. He was giving me good advice and getting me interviews with all of the best people in the business. When I had exhausted all of the magazine jobs, and I was in a lot of them back then, I started to focus on movies. Mike got me the opportunity to interview with a guy named Ruben who owned one of the most prestigious video companies at the time, called Vidco. I met with Ruben, who was an extremely professional man. He told me that from now on he was only shooting on video since it was going to be the wave of the future. I remember at the time it seemed silly. He was certainly right about this; I always say that porn is driven by technology. Whenever the technology advances so does the way that porn is delivered to the consumer.

The big thing back then was VHS. Remember back in the day, if you wanted to go see porn you had to actually enter a theater. This obviously was a big deal to the upstanding members of our society. You didn't want to hire a lawyer and then see him three seats over from you in a movie theatre jacking off. So now the lawyer could buy a tape and beat off in his own home while his wife was at bridge club. The only problem was, it was even harder to hide a VHS tape than a sticky magazine. That's when all off a sudden all sorts of porn tapes started showing up with labels written on them that said "family vacation" to throw girlfriends off the track.

People were starting to purchase VHS players and VHS tapes even though they started out rather expensive. Machines were selling for about $1,000.00 dollars and the porn VHS tapes were going for $99.99 and people were still buying them; remember this was the mid-'80's. Again, though, when you really think of it, can you put a price on being able to whack off to a video in the privacy of your own home? Obviously a lot of people didn't think so, because they were buying porn tapes at that price like crazy.

There was also a brief appearance of what was called laser disc. The quality of this was almost as good as 35mm film; in fact that was how they were created, so any porn that was shot on film could be transferred to laser disc. These were also pretty pricey and of course one had to have the laser disc player to watch it. In the early days VHS was a bit flat; it lost the three dimensional quality of film; the colors were often a bit weird, but it was fairly inexpensive to shoot, edit, replicate, box, market and distribute. The distribution was always where the porn biz had been walking a fine line, even before the invention of VHS.

The government during the Ronald Reagan administration had organized the Meese Commission, which was comprised of about twelve people whose sole job it was to view over 10,000 adult movies and create regulations on them. It goes without saying that the report was biased and inaccurate. Ed Meese was the attorney general at the time and in his own words the commission was formed to find "new ways to prevent the problems of pornography." Biased much?

At the end of viewing all this porn, I am surprised that the Meese commission was even able to speak and that their brains had not turned into mush. Their final opinions were written down in a document that was almost 2,000 pages long. That's right: a government commission wrote 2,000 pages about porn at the taxpayers' expense. They decided all sorts of fascinating things such as that is was legal to shoot porn where it was already legal to shoot porn but not any place where it wasn't. This left out LA, because it was illegal to shoot porn there. They decided that it was legal to possess it as long as it was within community standards. (Which community were they talking about, though: New York City or Mobile, Alabama?)

. Among the guidelines included were that everyone in a porn movie had to be over 18 years old and that there were to be no animals involved. (I think that we can all be cool with those two, even without the government telling us.) They also concluded that no foreign objects were to be inserted into assholes or vaginas, and that no actors or actresses were to be bound while they were having sex. (Okay, now it sounds like they are trying to ruin a good time.) They required there was to be no insertion of more than four fingers past the last knuckle (because everyone knows that fisting is just plain obscene). I also recall they were completely down on people getting pooped on for some odd reason.

Basically it was the Meese commission's job to decided what was obscene and what was not obscene and it took them looking at over 10,000 adult movies to figure this out. You just simply have to love the government at work for you. The other big thing that the Meese commission decided was that though the X-rated movies were legal to make, it was illegal to ship this obscene material across state lines. So basically go ahead and make it, just don't try to sell it.

This was obviously the greatest challenge for porn producers. Although most of the producers were located in LA, some were still on the East coast In New York City. The challenge would be shipping the VHS tapes across the country to the various adult bookstores were they could then be sold. In the old days of 35mm film, I can remember that the film cans were shipped around in anonymous unmarked vans. When I was working at the Cinema X, and the film delivery vans arrived, the whole building would go on lock down until the new film cans were delivered and the old films cans were picked up ready to be delivered to the next theater, so the films were being hand delivered, not sent through any type of mail system. Obviously this was to insure that the films were protected and not confiscated by any law enforcement as they crossed state lines, and they most certainly *did* cross state lines.

This system worked fine for the films which were being sent around to different theaters where they would play on the big screen for about two or three weeks, before they were switched out with another film. However, this system was not going to work for VHS tapes. First of all, there were going to be thousands of VHS tapes that would need to be delivered to hundreds of book and porn stores all over the country. They couldn't possibly fit in vans; semi-trucks would be needed, or the use of some sort of conventional delivery service. Using the United States Postal Service was dicey at best; UPS was a big risk as well.

The producers used whatever means they could to get the tapes from the production site to the bookstores. The ridiculous thing was that it was legal to make it, legal to sell it, legal to possess it but not legal to ship it. Obviously the Meese commission knew they would not be able to control porn based on the United States' constitutional 1st amendment rights. They knew the only way to control porn would be through shipping laws. The only problem with this is that where there's a will, there's a way. Anytime someone has something to sell and people who want to buy it, the two parties will find a way to make it happen. That's capitalism, baby.

So back to my piece of capitalism with Ruben, who gave me my first on-camera job in December of 1985. The name of the movie was *Depraved Innocent*; the script was a whole twenty pages long. It was being shot in San Francisco to avoid the illegality of shooting in LA. I got on a flight with Pacific Southwest Airlines, which was otherwise known as PSA. PSA airlines later came to be known as Porn Star Airlines within our circle because of the frequency that porn stars were flying up to San Francisco to shoot movies. I arrived at the hotel where all of the porn stars were staying, and over the evening I met several of the people that I would be working with the next day. Or to be more precise I met people that I would be sucking and fucking the next day. As time went on this became quite normal for me, but this day I remember thinking about how the very next day I would be fucking all of these people. It excited me, it did not scare me, and that all by itself took care of a lot of the jitters.

The next morning I had an early call time of eight in the morning. I arrived at the set, and soon met the director, who was an English bloke by the name of Jonathan Burroughs. He wasn't a famous director, but he wasn't a rookie either. He proceeded to walk me through the day and what was expected of me. Then it was off to makeup and soon I was in front of the camera for my first scene, which I really don't remember to this day.

I think that I was somewhat stunned. Which probably either made me more fun to fuck or less, depending on your attitude. I remember the movie was supposed to be a surrealistic dream thing; I had a girl-on-girl scene with Tracy Adams who was a super hot brunette that made a ton of movies back then and was quite well known. I do remember that there was an orgy scene with the whole cast at the end of the day of shooting. Yes, I said "day of shooting"; it was all done in one day. This was one of the big advantages to shooting on VHS; it was quick, really quick, which made it cost effective. Instead of taking one or two weeks to shoot 35mm film, VHS was being shot anywhere from one to four days. Everything went fairly well I am sure, but the thing I remember the most was that I was super nervous about the whole thing.

My mind was filled with all kinds of crazy voices, Was I going to be good enough, was I sexy enough, or pretty enough, or skinny enough, were my blowjobs going to be good enough, was my ass hot enough, was I going to moan good enough when I got fucked. The only way I got through the all the nervousness was to focus on the fact that I truly honestly loved sex and that I believed it would definitely show in the finished product.

That was the thing. I really liked to fuck and still do. The thought of banging all of these people at once didn't make me feel exploited and it didn't make me feel cheap. It made me excited. I'd watched enough porn to know that when a girl really enjoyed what she was doing it showed on film. All too often I had watched girls having sex, with that distant stare in their eyes looking up at the ceiling and wondering what color it should be painted. Or even worse were the ones that tried to act like they were into it by moaning and groaning but watching if you could tell they were just faking it. It was like they were being paid by the hour. It wasn't like that for me, and I never turned in a scene where I looked like a department store mannequin. Even that first day I was excited and I was into it.

I knew beyond a shadow of a doubt that my experience in the business would always be true and honest to myself and the minute that I hated what I was doing, I would stop. There was no amount of money that was worth selling my sexual soul for. I was not a victim and never would be one.

3

So it had begun. I was now in my first adult movie and there was no turning back. It was a huge relief when my first movie was done, I was so happy to not be that girl anymore that had never done it before. I was soon looking forward to the next one. The business is funny that way. It is sort of like a club. It is hard to get into it but once you are allowed past the gates things get much easier. I had no trouble finding work.

There were plenty more movies offered to me right away. I had the chance to work with some truly wonderful people. I soon got a job working with the famous porn director Anthony Spinelli, in a movie called *I Wanna be a Bad Girl*. In this movie I had the pleasure of having sex with Tommy Byron for the very first time. Tommy was funny because always he played the innocent teen that was being seduced well into his forties. I fucked him and Colleen Brennan in a bathtub. I believe that it was one of the last movies she performed in. Fucking them both was as fabulous as it sounds.

Everyone loved working for Spinnelli, for many reasons, He was a really cool guy and a great director. His movie *Nothing to Hide* is considered one of the all time classics and is loosely based on *Of Mice and Men*. If that doesn't tell you how cool he is nothing will. Who bases a porno on *Of Mice and Men*? The biggest reason that everyone loved working for him was because his wife made the best Italian food for everyone on the set. Usually we would have some horrible catered food brought in. But with Spinnelli we had, pasta marinara, antipasti, and all sorts of delicious things. It was the best food I ever had on any porn set.

I was starting to get regular work quite easily and things were going well. I became more comfortable with each film. Before long Ruben asked me to sign a contract with Vidco, this was in 1986. I remember this moment because it coincided with a big moment in history; the date that he asked me to sign was January 26, 1986. When I arrived at Ruben's office for our meeting he called me into the room with a casual invitation, saying, "Hey come on in, lets watch the shuttle launch before we start." We watched the shuttle take off; it went shooting up into the crystal blue sky and then it seemed to disappear into a puff of white smoke. I asked him, "Umm, is that supposed to happen?" Ruben said, "No, I don't think so kid." It was at that point that the newscaster announced that something awful had happened to the space shuttle Challenger and they were going to cut away for a break. Later we found out that the Challenger had exploded killing everyone on board. That was a sobering moment for me. I couldn't sign the contract that day. My head was a complete mess.

Ruben agreed to let me think it over until we got back from the CES show in Chicago in June, which gave me almost five months to consider it. The CES show was kind of odd. It stands for Consumer Electronics Show, which is all it was when it started out as but as time went on being present at the trade show became one of the biggest porn promotional tools in the business. What started as a show to promote electronic gadgets turned into something that was one of the biggest porn promotional tools in the business.

I worked for Ruben quite a few more times. Early in 1986 I did a movie called *Jane Bond meets Octopussy*, where I did a girl-on-girl scene with a beautiful Asian named Krista Barrington. This was back in the day when porn was over the top and funny. You know "Jane Bond, agent 0069," etc.

The movie also starred Amber Lynn, who was one of my idols along with Ginger Lynn. They were both originators in porn; they were really The New Generation. They were drop dead gorgeous outrageous bodies and they loved sex. What more could you want, really? When I was faced with the task of coming up with a porno name, I used the porno name formula, first you pick your favorite person or thing for your first name and then second you pick your favorite person or thing for last name. For example my best friend from Lansing took her favorite thing, which is Angels and then used the name of her best friend Kelly and became Angel Kelly. Another girlfriend took Tina Turner/Steven Tyler and became Tina Tyler; I think you get the idea. My favorite thing was a Porsche and my favorite porn stars being Amber/Ginger, so I became Porsche Lynn.

A lot of people think that either Ginger or Amber is my sister but no…I just picked the name.

There are some movies out there with me performing under the name Porsche/Portia Carrington. The TV show *Dynasty* was very big at the time, and everyone kept telling me how classy I was so I used that name for a bit.

I recall another movie I did for Vidco; the title escapes me right now but the experience does not. It involved houseboats. Vidco thought that a good way to get around the illegality of shooting in LA was to rent some houseboats in Sacramento and shoot porn on them. It was pitched to the porn stars as an exotic vacation for porn stars, they would be renting luxury house boats in the Sacramento delta for us to live on, there would be tanning, swimming and sex, what more could a porn star want? Doesn't that sound lovely? Of course it does, right?

Let me tell you there was no luxury about this event, in fact it was a fucking nightmare. When we arrived on the houseboats, we realized that apparently someone had switched out our luxury houseboats for what were basically floating house trailers. The plumbing sucked, and the food was horrible. I recall canned spaghetti being the best it got, and the water was an odd shade of green, which everyone was afraid to swim in. The only thing that was really there was the sun. Also of course once we were there we were pretty much trapped, it wasn't like we could just drive the thing to shore or anything.

The best thing about this experience was the fact that even though I was stuck in Hell, I was stuck there with some hot men. There was Hershel Savage, the epitome of tall dark and handsome, and also Eric Edwards, another totally hot kind of Robert Redford-type porn star. There was always a little bit of a silver lining, if I just looked for it. Every time I see Herschel Savage, we always comment about the time we were stuck on those houseboats in the Sacramento delta. It was odd; one might think that after fucking on film all day the last thing we would want to do when done would be to fuck more. But we did.

Things were going were well for the most part, and life was good. I was getting lots of work and had a good relationship with a hot older man who took good care of me. My boyfriend Mike was a Vietnam vet who suffered from a serious case of posttraumatic disorder, from the horrors he had witnessed. He was a kind gentle soul for the most part, but sometimes when he got drunk he changed. I could look into his eyes and I could see that the Mike I knew was not in there anymore.

He was a helicopter pilot in Vietnam who had flown helicopter gunships; he flew Hueys and Cobras, and his main job was raining down death from above. The good thing for him was that he wasn't on the ground mixed up with the hand-to-hand combat, but he was the one who came in to clean up and pick up during or after battles. It was his job to drop as many bombs and rockets as he could, and spray machine gun fire as much as humanly possible on the enemy and then pick up the extremely wounded off the jungle floor and get them to a hospital. So it goes without saying that he saw some really fucked up shit. It also goes without saying that he was damaged from this experience beyond belief. He was a good dude but he went on a wild ride. And it showed. Sadly, he was also someone who was not interested in really healing. It was easier for him to remain a victim of life's circumstances. I have a saying, "Your life's circumstances are not your life."

Vietnam would have been a lot worse if not for our helicopter pilots; they were amazing men, who flew hundreds of hours over their limit in conditions that no sane person would ever consider doing. I had come from a long line of military men in my family, my father was a master gunnery Sergeant, USMC, in Korea; he was heavily decorated, so I had and will always have a soft spot for marines and the military in general. I have had the pleasure of being with lots of military men, in relationships as well as one-night stands. I am always attracted to men with power and strength, and I certainly have some daddy issues as well. Although I have done a lot of work on all of my issues, I still love a good Daddy fuck. I love it when someone is fucking me and they say something like, "Who's your Daddy?"

Mike was prone to bouts of depression and nightmares and I was always trying to heal the part of him that was broken, which I never really accomplished. I adored him as he did me, but we were both working too hard to heal each other. This relationship hit its breaking point one night in Chicago. Mike and I were in Chicago for the CES convention. He was doing his thing and I was doing mine while we were there, but we were very much a couple and everyone around us knew it. I had been with him for a while and was as happy as I imagined I could be.

It was my first time signing autographs at a convention. I was signing for Vidco at their booth. I could hardly believe that people were actually willing to stand in line for my autographed picture. It was amazing to me that some of these people actually knew who I was. Mike was doing some of his own business. I usually went back to the hotel at night to get some rest for the next day and Mike would often go out in the evening for business dinners. A day of signing autographs consisted of being at the booth by ten in the morning, which meant getting up about seven to be showered, makeup and dressed to be at the booth at ten. It is actually an arduous task. People have no idea how much energy it takes to stand in six-inch heels, for eight hours, smiling, posing for photos and signing about 1,000 autographs. It really takes it out of you. Trust me.

One night Mike decided to go out with some friends for business drinks, I was tired and stayed at the hotel. I crashed out early after having a glass of wine and watching some TV. After a deep sleep I was awoken early in the morning with Mike coming into the room, he was cursing, yelling and screaming about something. This type of thing had happened before. I tried to smooth out the situation but he wasn't having it. He started to throw a fit in the room; he started freaking right the fuck out. He picked up the TV and threw it through the window, and began kicking over tables and chairs. As I was trying to pick up some of the things off the floor, Mike swung a large ceramic lamp around and made solid contact with my head. I will never forget the sound that it made.

The impact was painful, I saw stars, and it was a serious jolt to my body and to my mind. I sunk to the floor to assess if anything was broken, and it was then that I felt a gush of liquid starting to cover my face. At first I thought the liquid was water that somehow the lamp broke and water came out of it and then I realized it was actually blood that was gushing from a cut to my head. A head wound bleeds like crazy; I completely freaked out and ran out of the room into the hallway naked screaming for help. The amazing part was that several people opened their doors, saw me and then closed again. I guess they just didn't want to get involved with a crazy naked girl, whose face was covered in blood. Or maybe it was just the shock of it and the fact that all they had to do was close the door and the naked, bleeding screaming girl would go away.

Thank god there was one woman who worked for Vidco on the same floor who woke and did actually come to my rescue. She brought me into her room got me safe, got me some clothes to wear, a towel to stop the blood and made sure that I got to the hospital.

I will never forget lying on the table in the hospital crying, talking to the doctor about how I got the cut next to my eye. I was still trying not to get Mike in trouble so I was covering up for him; I told the doctor that I had slipped in the tub. The doctor wasn't buying it and tried to get me to tell him the truth but I couldn't do it. No matter what Mike had just done we still had a code, we had been partners in crime for a long time. He told me that the cut was deep and was going to have to be irrigated and then stitched. Tears were streaming down my face, I explained to him that I made my living from my face, which was sort of true anyway, and could he please do a good job stitching it up. He said that I was in luck because he had a colleague who was still on duty who was a plastic surgeon and he would see if the other doctor would be able to stitch the cut up for me. The plastic surgeon came in and worked on the cut, which was right on the temple above my left eye. The cut was deep and jagged, the doctor explained that he would do the best job he could do however, I may experience some nerve damage and what he termed a lazy eye reaction from the injury.

Oh great, porn stars with lazy eyes were all the rage. I certainly wasn't going to be signing autographs the next day. I also probably wasn't going to be the first famous porn star with a lazy eye. Thank God this didn't happen but at the time I was terrified.

All I could think about was getting out of Chicago, and getting away from Mike. I wanted to go back to LA as soon as possible so I could move out of the house and get a place of my own. There had been many similar situations to this one over the years that we had been dating, usually alcohol and drug induced. When they happened they just sort of seemed like bad dreams, I would wake up the next day and he would be sleeping beside me, and it was all okay, like nothing had gone on.

I had always confronted Mike saying that someday he was going to hurt me and he needed to get help for his problems. He promised me that he would never hurt me, even in the tornado of destroying things, yelling and screaming, I had sat on the floor with bottles, dishes flying by my head very nearly hitting me. I had believed him that he would never hurt me, not intentionally anyways. Of course there was the inevitable possibility that someday something would go wrong and of course it did. He swung a lamp and hit me in the fucking head with it. Of course I didn't have the wisdom to leave before it happened. But now that it had I was gone.

4

This incident with Mike forced me into action. I was not interested in being a victim. I quickly got an apartment back home, and moved out before Mike returned home from Chicago. At this point I realized that there was no way that I could ever sign a contract with Vidco, that would just keep me too close to Mike. I decided that I would most certainly be signing with a company called Dino Ferrari instead.

I was seeking sanctuary for myself from all the fear, the pain and the hurt. This incident brought up all kinds of unhealed issues for me, all the issues with my father and men in general were right in my face and they weren't pretty. When I was seven years old my father shot my mother, in front of my Grandmother and me. He later shot himself. Needless to say this left me completely broken and with many issues that required healing at some point. I was on my path to recovery but wasn't there quite yet.

I was broken in so many ways after what happened with Mike. I felt betrayed and abused both physically and spiritually. I needed to be alone and I needed to be on my own. He was the love of my life, or so I thought. What I failed to realize was that I had basically fallen in love with a man that was just like my father. What the fuck was I thinking? What a shock it was to become his victim. I still think of him as a good man. He was always fighting demons and that night they won.

Lenny was the guy in charge of Dino Ferrari Productions and he took good care of me. I signed a contract with him to work exclusively for his company. It was a popular trend back in the day for big XXX movie producers and studios to sign popular female porn stars to contracts.

The advantage to this was that the studio could insure that porn star only worked for them, they had a face to market and brand. It was mostly a gimmick but one that was successful. Marilyn Chambers was the first person to sign a contract with the Mitchell brothers, and then Ginger Lynn signed with Vivid. The contract thing had worked out pretty good for both of them and it seemed like a good way for me to go. The advantage for the girl was that she had a guaranteed monthly income from the company, as well as a marketing machine behind her and she didn't have to search for work anymore. It really was a win/win for both parties.

Lenny B was super good to me; he was very respectful and professional. The unique thing about Lenny was that he had offices in Europe and had decided that the way to get around the shooting laws in LA was to take porn stars to Europe and shoot the movies there. That's what the man did; he literally hired about six porn stars as well a top-notch director and a few cameramen and flew all of us to Europe.

My first trip was to Germany to shoot a movie called *Club Taboo*. The cast was Nina Hartley, Colleen Brennan, Joey Silvera, John Leslie and also several German porn stars. The director was Henri Pachard; he was very famous from the 35mm days. Lenny B was shooting on VHS like most everyone else these days but was trying desperately to keep the quality of the production up, with great scripts, sets, expensive wardrobes and so on. Most of the time, he hit the mark; his movies always had an air of French au vanguard, and they had the Fellini thing going with the addition of the exotic European talent, outrageous sets, costumes & makeup. It was a crazy time. I felt like a big shot, a true movie star.

What porn star didn't want to go to Europe to shoot porn? Seriously! It was the best escape from reality that I could get.

Shooting porn in Europe was a trip! That's the best way I can explain it. My first trip to Europe was to Germany, and I want to go back to that a bit. You have to remember that I was born and raised in Michigan and had barely traveled the USA. I had never been out of the country, although I had always wanted to travel to Europe and at one time my college sweetheart and I considered a cycling over there. I did end up riding around on a lot of things while I was in Europe but not many bicycles.

My first trip to Europe was first class. I flew from LAX to Munich then onto the smaller town of Hamburg. As I said there were several other porn stars traveling as well, Colleen Brennan, Nina Hartley, John Leslie and myself. We were housed in a very quaint cottage-like hotel, which was very sweet except for the fact that there was nothing around for miles.

John Leslie made the remark that maybe they were hiding us so no one knew we were in the country. The cottage hotel happened to be very close to the film studios where we would be shooting. This studio was then owned by a couple, Hans and Teresa Orlowski; it was very large and impressive, a bit like Teresa, who had the largest breasts on the smallest body frame that I had ever seen. I always sort of wanted to play with them. She was a beautiful buxom brunette porn star who was quite famous in Europe, apparently for more than her huge knockers. We shot several films on their set while I was in Europe.

The best story I have from this experience: I was shooting a scene with Joey Silvera; we were in a large, opulent bathroom, with several urinals, toilets, bidets and so forth. I was dressed in a black leather skirt, a black leather bolero jacket, black leather 6-inch stilettos and a black bolero hat, looking very much the typical dominant, aggressive female. Remember it was late '80s-early '90s which did not give us the most sensible fashions to say the least. Sometimes when I look back at these movies and see the hair and the clothes I am wearing it is hard not to laugh. Joey and I had discussed the scene that we were about to do. We were talking about how the set was going to be this bathroom, into which I had followed Joey with the plan of fucking him after he used the toilet.

Whatever! We always had to have some silly lead-in to a sex scene; I never understood why it was that people just couldn't decide to fuck. I mean instead of me just making out with him or starting to suck his cock I decided that I would just follow him into the shitter. Makes sense, right?

Joey and I had worked out a scene that we thought would be hot and that would be fun for us. Joey knew that I enjoyed bondage and domination and I knew that he did as well. So we decided to do a kind of Domination scene, where I entered the bathroom and proceeded to basically dominate Joey into fucking me. Well you know what I say: you can't rape the willing, can you darlings? Joey asked if I would be willing to chain his hands through the bidet plumbing, because he thought it would be kind of cool if he were chained up, bound and helpless. The funny thing was that I also thought it would be kind of cool if he were chained bound and helpless.

Joey managed to get a small set of chains from someone on the set and we made ready to start the scene. The director as I said was Henri Pachard, who was known for his kinky tendencies; as a matter of fact he had been making kinky movies since the '60s so we knew that it wasn't going to be a hard sell on him. Joey and I sold Pachard on the idea and the cameras began to roll. I walked onto the set, and stepped close to Joey and backed him up against the wall. I placed my hand around his throat and my other hand between his legs, gripping his cock hard. I placed my lips on his and kissed him deeply and passionately. I told him to sit on the bidet, lifted my skirt up, and was standing before him with no panties on. I then ordered him to lick my pussy. He did so like a good slave would. I was turned on as hell.

The sex moved forward with Joey completely surrendering to me in every way. It was hot and steamy; it was raw and very real. We were aware that we were 100 percent in the zone because the film crew was completely quiet, you could hear a pin drop. There was no input from the director, lighting guy or the boom guy. I was totally in the moment. Joey sat completely naked on the bidet, me still standing in front of him with only black silk stockings, garter belt and black stilettos on, I grabbed the chain quickly wrapped it around his hands and then around the plumbing above the bidet. He looked so hot, naked, his body glowing with a sweat, his hands chained above his head and his cock rock hard. I went to my knees and sucked his dick until I couldn't take it anymore, I stood up and quickly mounted his cock, and I was fucking him hard and fast. I became slightly aware of some talking in the background but nothing was going to keep me off of Joey's cock at this point.

The talking increased behind us and it started to sound angry. A lot of it was in German, which I didn't speak, so I had no idea what they were saying. And then right in the middle of my orgasm I heard the dreaded words "CUT! NIN, NIN, NIN," which is "No" in German, if you don't speak German either. The director walked onto the set and told me that I had to unchain Joey's hands if we were to continue shooting. I was a real rebel at this point in my life, so I asked, "What the fuck? Why do I have to unchain him?" The director explained that the Germans were afraid of shooting sex and bondage, because technically it was illegal. Apparently Henri was made aware of this from a few members of the German crew while Joey and I were fucking.

Again I asked, "What the fuck?" I had seen a lot of German porn with all kinds of disgusting acts that even I wouldn't partake in, things like sex with animals for example. When I said this to him, Henri explained that none of the animals were tied up. Oh my fucking god, you have got to be kidding me! You could make porn with animals but you couldn't chain someone up and fuck them? Even if the person was totally willing to have this happen and be fucked in that manner? Really? Okay, so it's cool to fuck an animal as long as you don't tie it up. Great. I unchained Joey but he insisted on leaving the chain wrapped around he wrist as he continued to fuck me and end with the money shot, which as most of you know is the cum shot in porn. This wasn't professional anymore, this was personal.

The next trip to Europe was Paris, the city of love. I knew I had finally hit the big time. There were costume fittings and scripts were a hundred pages long. This was the real deal.

This trip consisted of myself, and a bunch of other miscreants. I was with Paul Thomas, Jamie Gillis, and my personal favorite Ty Randolph, who was thought of as a straight actress that didn't do such things; to this day I am not really sure what she was doing there. We also were with the American director Jack Remy who was a long-term pro in the porn business. It really is amazing how many people I worked with in those early days became icons in the business.

We were put up in the grandest hotel on one of the most fabulous streets in the world, the Champs Élysées; I must say it was all very impressive. But still at the end of the day, we were making porn, with all of its up and downs, no pun intended. The mission was to shoot two films; the first was *Mimi, an American Girl in Paris* and also *The Girl with the Million Dollar Legs*. We were going to be using a lot of French porn stars, like Marilyn Jess, Gabriel Pontello and Christopher Clark. It was fun meeting the French porn stars and a bit challenging as well. Trying to do a sex scene with people who spoke little or no English was not always the easiest thing. One would think it wouldn't matter but when a strange woman started licking your pussy, at times it still got a little confusing. There are a lot of things that get lost in translation in such situations.

The best part of shooting in Paris was the wine. We often used locations such as houses, so our breakfasts and lunches were almost always catered. There were always bottles of wine on the catering table even as early as 7:00 AM. The lunch boxes consisted of a small sandwich, salad, and small bottles of red and white wine, with a liqueur of some sort. I love wine, so having it available all day long was a good thing. Seven days and seventy bottles of wine, and a lot of fucking later, the movies were finished. I am surprised I remember any of it.

The folks at my movie company informed me that they had taken out an insurance policy on my legs, just like Betty Grable. Betty Grable was known as the "*girl with the million dollar legs*, she got a lot of mileage out of it. My company took out a one million dollar policy on my legs from Lloyds of London. They assured me it was mostly a publicity stunt and that they hoped we never had to cash in on it. Yeah, let's hope so. I was a tad disappointed that he didn't insure my vagina but you know what can I say. I became known as the girl with the million dollar legs. Imagine being known as "The Girl with the Million Dollar Pussy." I bet you could get a lot of mileage out of that too. As a matter of fact the movie that I just mentioned called *The Girl With the Million Dollar Legs* was sort of designed around me. It was the biggest movie in my new career. The publicity was off the charts. The next convention I went to involved me signing huge posters as the girl with the million dollar legs. Now I think about it, I'm glad he didn't do the vagina thing.

The Girl With the Million Dollar Legs had a marketing monster behind it. I don't know if my legs were as good as Betty Grable's but it was a huge compliment to be compared to her in any way, shape or form. The box cover for the movie was a photo of me, naked except for an incredible pairs of heels, legs up in the air and important bits covered up with a black feather boa.

The next European trip would take us to Italy; Rome to be exact.. The ancient city of pasta, amour and wine. Italy was still using lira as currency; a Coca-Cola was 6,000 lire, equivalent to six dollars, and a Chianti was 600 lire, equivalent to one dollar. Now which one are you going to drink, really? It was so sad to be forced to drink Chianti all the time.

This trip brought together some of my favorite porn stars, such as John Leslie, Barbara Dare, Joey Silvera, Sharon Mitchell; all of them the best of the best. The movies that we made there were *Barbara Dare's Roman Holiday, Grand Prixxx*, and *When In Rome*. This trip was very fun, the Italian porn stars were super sweet to us, they were always taking us out to the best discos in Rome. We spent much of our time dancing and drinking the nights away. We were making porn on a boat, because technically it wasn't legal to make porn in Italy but it wasn't technically illegal either. This was also when Ciccolina, the Italian porn star, was running for a parliament position and actually won. In some odd way we all felt a little bit close to her for doing so at the time.

It was on one of these boats while we were filming that Sharon Mitchell and myself had the pleasure of meeting the young hot actor Rocco Siffredi for the first time. He was an amazingly good-looking young man; tall, handsome as the day is long and extremely well built, everywhere. In other words, his cock was huge. Now obviously as porn stars we were used to huge cocks. But there is "oh my!" huge and then there is "Oh my fucking god, I think I am going to heaven" huge. Rocco's cock was of the latter persuasion.

Sharon Mitchell, who was known as Mitch to her good friends, had the pleasure of working with him for the first time. When I say "the pleasure of working with him" what I mean is that she basically had a fire hydrant shoved up her pussy. The rest of us watched the monitors while the scene was being filmed and stood in awe of the size of his cock. Oh my fucking god, I was terrified. The first problem was that Rocco spoke not one word of English, so Mitch couldn't tell him to slow down, change the position, or add some more lube. Everything that Mitch said to him fell on deaf ears. Rocco had absolutely no foreplay game meaning there was no kissing, fingering, oral, etc. He was all game. The scene went basically like this: Mitch walked up to Rocco on the boat; Rocco smiles, bends Mitch over and starts fucking her. I know it may seem to many of you that this is the basic recipe for porn, when that is often all you see in the finished product, the foreplay having been left on the cutting room floor.

My scene with Rocco came a few days later in a cold castle outside of Rome. I told the director Fred Lincoln to tell Rocco that I would need a good warm up before actual penetration. I overheard Freddy telling Rocco, "Amore, Rocco, Amore, you understand?" Rocco responded in stumbled English, "Ci, ci, amore, ci." I thought, okay, it seems that we have an understanding. The scene took place on a bed. I was dressed in red: bra, panties, high-heeled pumps and red gloves with a red leather dress. I did my best to seduce Rocco. At the beginning of the scene, he grabbed me and threw me down on the bed, licked my pussy a few times in a very nonchalant way and immediately tried to stick his big fat cock into me. I screamed "Cut" at the top of my lungs, bringing the scene to a halt. Rocco gave me a confused look. He actually looked a little hurt. This surprised me I must say. I would imagine that someone with such an enormous cock would be used to this by now. I tried to tell him that my pussy needed to be wet before he stuck his cock in. He seemed to get it. The only way this was going to happen was by me using a huge glop of abolene, which was the preferred choice of lube in those days. I slathered his cock with the thick lube and went back at it. The scene ended up being pretty good, amazingly enough, right down to the oral cum shot on my red gloves. At the end of the scene, Freddy asked me what I thought about Rocco; my response was, "Well, I think the kid will be a big star someday." I was right about this. The guy is huge in Italy and everywhere else, no pun intended. He grew to be a suave porn star and an all-around great guy. He and his huge cock have made a ton of money, a ton of movies and he even now stars in some potato chip commercials in Italy.

While I was in Rome making porn, I was told by several people to be careful of the burro. I wasn't sure quite what to make of it. I thought that burro meant butter, so I thought that people were telling me to be careful of using butter as a lube in porn. Which still didn't make a lot of sense but what did I know? I found out later that they were actually referring to the animal burro, and making burro films. Like, people were actually warning me not to let a burro fuck me! Luckily, I never had a burro as a co-star.

We also had the pleasure of shooting a movie on Mario Andretti's racetrack with a formula one car. Okay, so none of us were really able to drive the car, but being on the track watching the cars zip by, hearing the engines racing, was a total rush. John Leslie was able to get behind the wheel of one of the cars while they pulled it around the track. I have never seen John so happy in all of my life. What guy wouldn't want to be behind the wheel of a formula one car? We weren't able to actually fuck in the car so we opted for fucking on top of the car; the crew was super scared that I was going to scratch the paint with my stiletto heels. My response was, "I'm not going to scratch the paint with my heels, and I'm a professional here." And I didn't.

One time I was shooting a scene that involved me and a gorgeous Italian guy who didn't speak English. I asked my director Fred Lincoln how was I supposed to communicate with this guy about the scene if he didn't' speak a word of English? Fred was a true professional, he had been around a long time and told me to feel my way through the scene and just use what I knew. At the time I spoke about three words in Italian, none of which were going to help me in a porn scene. The scene was shot in a restaurant with a huge Italian meal on the table. The idea was that we were supposed to being having dinner and we become overcome with passion, and wind up fucking on the table of food. The scene developed slowly with lots of kissing, heavy petting above and below the waist, my personal favorite. I pulled up my skirt, pushed the guy face into my pussy saying, "Mange, mange, mange," which is Italian for eat. The guy looked up at me like I was crazy. I heard Fred laughing out loud on the set with the whole crew. It's always a good thing when you hear the director and crew laughing on a porn set.

Another story that always makes me laugh was shooting in France with Henri Pachard and one of my favorite cameramen whose name was JD. He was the DP (Director of Photography), which is kind of an inside joke because in porn "DP" refers to double penetration, usually where a girl takes one cock in her pussy and one cock in her ass simultaneously, but it can also be taking two cocks in the pussy or two cocks in the ass. No, I have never taken two in either. The scene was with myself, an actress named Bionca and Joey Silvera. Bionca was at one point married to the famous porn director Bruce Seven.

The set up for the scene was Bionca playing a woman who was totally afraid to be seen having sex. She was so freaked out by this that she had nightmares while having sex that there were hundreds of people standing around watching her and staring at her while she was trying to screw. The point was that she was unable to have sex because of this phobia. Joey and I were to play therapists that were going to "assist" her with this problem. In other words we were going to fuck her. But of course our lovely patient Bionca had no idea about this at this time.

I walked onto the set and the first thing that I saw was the production manager gluing plastic eyeballs on a wall, on a coffee table, a lamp shade, and so on. I asked what she was doing and she said that the eyeballs were to represent the people that were watching Bionca's character have sex. Okay. That sounds hot, right? I mean this is a porno, are we trying to turn people on or freak them out? There was even a bunch of plastic eyeballs on the couch where the sex scene was going to happen. I started thinking about these and what I was going to do with them in the scene. I thought about putting them in Bionca's pussy and asshole. The funniest thing I thought that somewhere out there would be some dude watching the movie that would blow his load right when I shoved one of these eyeballs right in her ass and he wouldn't even know why.

I thought about it more and decided maybe that wasn't a good idea after all. They were about the size of large Ben Wa balls, which were metal balls; an Asian invention for exercising the pussy muscles, so I thought maybe it would be safe to stick them in Bionca's pussy. As the scene started rolling, Bionca was on her hands and knees sucking Joey's cock; I was licking her pussy and fingering her ass from behind, still thinking about the eyeballs, as they were everywhere. Bionca and I had worked together many times in the past and I knew that she was usually up for just about anything, especially if it involved something kinky, that would make a great scene.

I pick up one of the eyeballs and put it in her pussy. I don't think she was entirely sure what was going on but she pushed it out. This was not bad; it seemed like it worked pretty good. I was a true pro after all. Improvisation was my thing. I then slid one of the eyeballs into her ass and I left it so that it was just at the entrance. It looked like there was an eye looking out at me. I started laughing uncontrollably, but very softly under my breath. She was bucking, shaking and jiggling all around with this little eyeball staring out at me. The cameraman moved around behind me to get another shot and he started laughing softly as well. The next thing I knew Bionca coughed a bit from all the cocksucking and the eyeball flew out of her ass and almost hit the camera lens. I couldn't control it any longer, I burst out in laughter and so did JD and the rest of the crew. It will remain one of the best all-time bloopers in porn history.

Moments like that I will remember forever. Since then, every time I have seen JD, he reminds me of that scene and says he has never forgotten it either. Americans that traveled on these trips to Europe were responsible for impacting porn in Europe in a major way. We broke up the porn industry there, we built a bridge from American porn to European porn. All in all, it was an incredible time for a little girl from a small town in the USA, and I am grateful for the experience. It made me a star in Europe and paved the way for many future trips.

Overnight I was turned into a rock star. I rode in limousines and wore designer clothes. I stayed at the most expensive hotels, and I had access to all the alcohol & drugs I could consume. And I could consume a lot. I truly could. It was a magical time.

5

Porn was making one of the biggest transitions it would make in its history, it was moving out of theaters and into the homes of almost everybody on the planet. VCRs were coming down in price so more people were able to purchase them. The porn producers were learning how to shoot on VHS, making the product look better; we even shifted to beta max for a while, insisting that it was a better picture. For the people who couldn't afford a VCR and the porn videos, the adult bookstore accommodated. They were able to set up video viewing booths, where it became completely economical for the bookstore to build a bunch of small booths with a screen onto which they would show a porn video, the customer would place money, usually dollar bills or tokens into the machine and the video would run for a specific set of time. Excellent, right? What a great invention, we could finally jerk off in the privacy of a viewing booth instead of in a large theater, where some guy was bound to ask you if you needed help with that. I mean, I am sure there is nothing worse than almost getting off looking at a chick's gorgeous boobs in a porn theatre, and seeing out of the corner of your eye a little chubby weirdo who is getting off while looking at you beating off. I don't have to be a guy to imagine how much of a drag that would have been.

In essence, porn stars were moving out of the closet into the American public's bedrooms, living rooms, and the local adult bookstore. We were everywhere.

If one were to talk to a person in their twenties now about the way it used to be then, they would not believe it. There was a huge stigma attached to going into a porn theater in the first place. If you were a businessman in the community it could bring huge shame to you even being seen walking in the door; it was a big deal. People back then actually used to say things like "I saw Joey's dad going into the porn theatre." And then of course, what do you do when you watch porn? You beat off. It isn't like you just hang on to the memories for when you get home and jack off while your wife is sleeping next to you. So your choice back then, if you really wanted to watch some porn, was to face the stigma of walking into a porn theatre and beating off in public. Of course, in the larger cities it was possible to be somewhat incognito but not in the medium-sized cities or smaller towns. If you checked out porn, sooner or later someone knew. It is not possible to overstate how important it was for the porn business that people were able to partake in their own homes.

Porn stars were part of the 'it' factor of the '80s and the early '90s. We were really the rock stars of our time. We were famous for almost the same reasons, we were living lives others could only dream about, and we were all high on sex, drugs & rock and roll. Everybody either wanted to be us or get with us. I loved my life, even though at times it took on a surreal form. When one lives the way I was living, it becomes very hard to tell anymore what should be going on and what shouldn't. Everything just sort of happens and you don't think too much about it, you just don't want it to stop.

I only worked on a movie about five days out of the month. The rest of the time was mine to spend however I wanted, as long as I didn't shoot movies for anybody else. I still did some modeling, but decided that with all the free time I had that I was ready to go back to my roots, to go back to burlesque, back to the form that had brought me to where I was. I loved to dance, loved the party life of the clubs, loved traveling and I loved being in a different town every week.

The strip clubs were ready for something new; they welcomed the porn star to come to their clubs. It was quite the big promotion and quite the scene when I would come to town. They could charge a ton of money by having someone with my name come to their club and I made good money as well. My first big gig was at a place called the Million Dollar Saloon in Toronto Canada. *The Girl With the Million Dollar Legs* had just been released, although Canada was not getting much porn if any, which was a fact that I didn't know until I got there. I was warned about not taking any porn tapes across the border, which I abided by. The club held about 1500 people within and had a balcony; it was a huge state of the art strip club. Its stage was elevated about twenty feet in the air. It had a full liquor bar and full nudity was good to go there, as well as table dancing.

The size of the club was astounding; strip clubs owners were making a new trend of building huge gentlemen's clubs, complete with extremely opulent decorations. I think that they were trying to use the size of their strip club as a form of penis comparison. My club's bigger than yours. The other thing that stood out in Canada was the fact that the Canadians didn't have these weird laws regarding alcohol and nudity. In the states, the laws were very restrictive; the clubs could have full alcohol, meaning beer, wine and hard liquor which is my personal favorite, but the strippers needed to keep their bottoms on. Sometimes this meant a thong, other times it meant full bikini bottoms; sometimes we even had to have pasties over our boobs because you know if the nipples were viewed while drinking alcohol someone would really go over the edge. It could get ugly.

Again, this sounds silly but it was true. All over America poor horny drunk guys would go to strip clubs to see a girl dance who didn't even expose her entire breasts. I found this to be totally ridiculous. If you are going to go for it, then go all the way. What's the point otherwise? I really have a hard time believing that if a man views nudity while drinking liquor that somehow he will lose all control of his senses and harm himself or someone else.

The Canadians with all their wisdom did not buy into the bullshit; in Canada the clubs had beer, wine, alcohol and allowed full nudity on the stage. It was party time. They also allowed naked table dances even though the dancer had to dance on a wooden box which was about 3 ft x 3ft x 3ft. This wooden box became a portable stage thus the sneaky Canadians got around the law that all nudity needed to be on a stage. "What do you mean I'm not on a stage, officer? Can't you see the box I am standing on?"

The other nice thing about Canada was the additional shows that were possible; the Canadians were the first ones to get really creative with show possibilities. For example, I remember one of the acts opening up for me was a shower show. The customer would see a suspended glass shower over the stage, where 2 girls would perform a shower show together. This consisted of two totally hot girls getting naked in a hot shower, soaping each other up and spraying each other down. Again, the girl-on-girl sex could not be totally blatant, it had to be playboy style. You know where you see the girl's head between the other girl's legs; you see her head moving up and down and the other girl is moaning and groaning, so one assumes that something good is happening. This is what we call soft core porn, where you see naked people who look like they are doing something sexual but you don't ever see their private bits enter the other person's private bits.

I have to be honest, though, and say for a performer it wasn't any less awkward. At times it was more so. Imagine me on all fours with my face an inch away from another girl's pussy with me shaking my head around with my tongue out and her moaning and twitching like crazy without me even touching her. After a minute or two of that I truly would want to go down on the other girl, just so there would be a point to the whole thing.

The Canadians were the masters of girl-on-girl simulated sex shows; there would be shows in glass showers, girl-on-girl shows on stage, even on the three-by-three-by-three wooden box. Even in Canada there were some laws; for instance, it was the law that the dancing girls had to keep one article of clothing on, so we had breakaway thongs, these were thongs that had little clips on the sides which enabled you to clip them off with out bending over to take your bottoms off. We would then wrap that thong around either our ankle or wrist, in effect leaving one article of clothing on. So you know basically you could see right up inside of me, but my wrist was covered. Genius no? The other trick was to pull your boobies out of your top keeping the top on and then wrap the thong around your ankle. So I would be out there naked with my boobs shaking around and my womanhood hanging out, but it wouldn't be obscene because my shirt was rapped around my stomach and my thong was around my ankle.

Another law was that all dancing girls had to perform on a stage, so as I said before we had a small wooden box about 3'x3' that we would carry around the club. We would sell table dances where we would sit the wooden box down on the floor and dance on it. This meant that we were dancing naked, with our one article of clothing on about two inches from the customer. So again I am standing on a box with my thong around my ankle and a guy's face a couple of inches from my taco. But you know I'm on a stage and I am wearing clothes, right? One simply has to love the ingenuity of this. Who thinks of things like this? It's like there is some stripper evil genius that gets paid by the industry to figure out ways around all of the laws!

They were also masters of the truest form of burlesque; in fact they had been the ones keeping it alive over the years. Girls had been performing in Canada with huge burlesque shows for quite a while now; it was a big deal around there. There were often lots of pyrotechnics, and themed shows with girls on trapezes and such; some of these women even performed with animals. It was sort of like the circus except with naked chicks.

These women that performed in such shows were truly amazing performers. I was very impressed with their creative artistry. I stood backstage watching the first performer I ever saw at the Million Dollar Saloon; I believe her name was Carolyn Jones, who was a beautiful brunette with a banging figure and a sweet smile. She was an amazing dancer, and looked like she had probably been to a dance school of some type. After one of her songs, she walked off stage and stepped out of sight of everyone, when she returned to the stage she was walking a tiger down the stage runway. It was a gorgeous well behaved tiger but a tiger nonetheless. The place went crazy; money was flying onto the stage like it was raining dollar bills. For a little farm girl from Michigan this was an amazing sight. I was blown away.

When it came time for me to take the stage, I turned to the stagehand and asked him just how the fuck was I going to follow that? I mean this gorgeous chick was just out there; she danced like a professional from the New York City Ballet and then came back out with a tiger for fuck's sake! All I was planning on doing was doing a little dance and shaking my tits around for twenty minutes.

The stagehand looked as bewildered as I did. He shook his head and said "You're Porsche Lynn, maybe that will help." Hah, fat chance, since Canadians didn't even have porn videos yet. Most of them had no idea who I was. I took the stage anyway and stumbled my way through my set as best as possible. What I remember the most was being on the stage and over half of the people standing up and leaving. The stagehand told me not to take it personal since they just needed to go back to work. Oh, but they hadn't walked out on the girl with the tiger.. Well, I guess I wasn't the most famous thing on the planet. It was the first of many humbling experiences. I would have to work on not taking it personally. I think this was really good for me at the time. I was getting so used to adulation and being treated like a big star that having this happen was the right thing for me at the right time. We all need a good dose of humility now and then.

I am happy to say that my feature performances got better from here on in, because if they had continued to be anything like that, I would have probably have been tempted to slit my wrists in a cold, dark corner. They would have found me naked except with a thong wrapped around my ankle.

Early Modeling days 1983.

Early cheescake days,
1983, 21 years old

Cheri magazine shoot 1985

Angel Kelly & me getting ready for Mötley Crüe.

Shot from *Girl with the Million Dollar Legs.*

With one of the best,
Fred Lincoln.

First Movie, December 1985.

High Society photo by
Suze Randall, 1989.

Jerry Butler and I about to have a throw down.

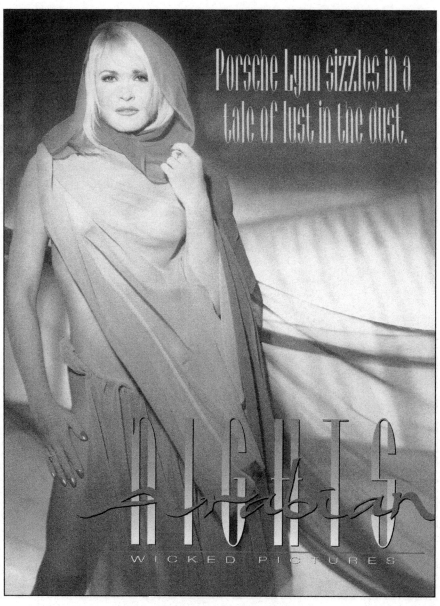

Movie with award winning DP scene.

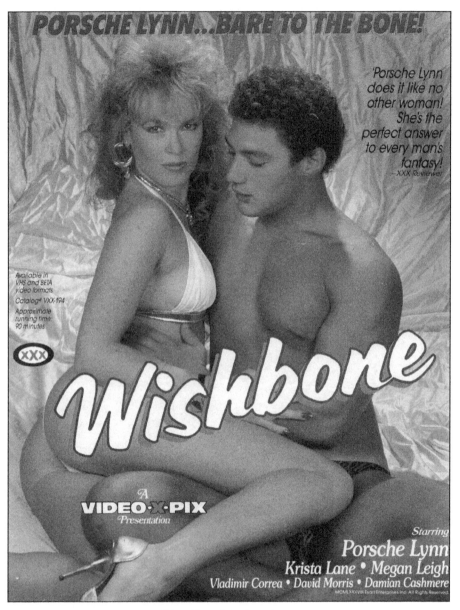

One of my favorite covers.

Test Shots for *Penthouse.*

Yes, this is really Moulin Rouge, Paris, 1987.

6

A s time went on I figured out that a better place to practice burlesque dancing was back in the good old USA. Porn was thriving and there were still places where sex shows and on stage nudity were legal. I told my burlesque agent that I wanted more work. Yes, there is truly an agent for everything. There is always someone there to get you work and take twenty percent of your earnings. As I was saying, I told my agent to book me at Show World in NYC and The Mitchell Brothers in San Francisco. These were probably my two most favorite cities in the USA; they both were still keeping it real when it came to sex.

I believe that I went to Show World first. So can I just say, oh my fucking god, New York City, 42nd Street, my name on the marquee, a *Girl With the Million Dollar Legs* poster on the front of the theater. This was the most magical place I had ever seen. It was also one of the strangest. What a blast the whole thing was!

I will always remember the first time I walked into the theater, it felt like I was like coming home. It brought me back to my roots. I was shot back to the Cinema X days. I loved these places, I truly did; they were the best of all worlds. There was dancing, loud music, naked bodies, and lots of sex everywhere. When you walked into Show World, it literally looked like a circus; there were lots of lights everywhere, the type of lights that looked like they belonged under the Big Top; there were carousel horses, and people milling about everywhere. There were three floors of everything you could imagine: chicks with dicks were hanging down in the basement, one-on-one peep booths, video viewing booths, an adult store with any sort of toys that one could imagine, as well as just tons of magazines and videos for sale.

51

On the third floor was the theater, called Triple Treat, which had about a hundred seats and it was rather small. They were typical theater seats, arranged around a stage that was about ten feet by twelve feet, and about two feet off the ground, a pretty close proximity to the audience. Movies would play and in between the movies, there were live shows on stage; it was very similar to what I did when I first got in the business. Sometimes they were just single girl shows, which involved dancing, stripping in the traditional manner. But then of course, just like in the old days at Cinema X, there would also be the floorshow. During the floorshow, the girl would usually do some type of masturbation show, often with dildos or other toys.

At show time there were often girl-on-girl shows. The crowd got a really hardcore version, you could see two girls licking each others' pussies, fucking each other with dildos, fisting and so on. Sometimes even there would even be guy-on-girl sex shows; these were real honest hardcore live sex shows. So basically a customer would watch a movie then two people would come out on the stage and fuck and then another movie would start. Did I mention that this place has been shut down?

When the porn stars did shows at Show World, the theater tried to play one of their movies before their performance so it created the effect of sitting in a theater watching a porn movie, a few minutes later the girl you saw getting fucked and sucking cock was dancing right in front of you. So basically they would show one of my movies and get people totally worked up, then I would come out and dance around and play with myself right in front of them. Great marketing, wouldn't you say?

As a performer, I was allowed to do anything at Show World that I wanted. I always did a little dancing, which I had gotten better at I must say. I then followed that up with a great floor and a fabulous masturbation show. This was my specialty; over the years I had perfected the ability to deep throat a large dildo, which always created a gasp from the audience. What can I say? Practice makes perfect.

The audience was always supportive, friendly and appreciative, and as kind as New Yorkers can be on any given day. It really was like a party in there. A phenomenon that was birthed from this was the Polaroid photos shoots that they did at the end of every show. When my show was finished, hopefully with me having at least one orgasm on stage, and I say that for my benefit, not for the crowds, I would pick up my tips on the stage, thank the audience and invite them to meet me in the lobby for autographed Polaroid photos.

Now again in today's day and age people are reading this and saying "what"? Who cares? But a Polaroid was such a big deal back then. I mean in a matter of seconds some dude could be walking away with a photo of me naked on his lap. He not only could whack off to it but he would be the envy of all his friends. Well at least the ones that he would dare show it to. This still goes on today with porn stars and strippers that travel around. Except that the cameras are digital and the images get downloaded to a device that prints the photos. A sad part of new technology taking over is that old technology will die, for instance, the Polaroid camera is no more; even if you do have a camera, its impossible to purchase film for it. I believe that the Polaroid Company was shut down a few years ago. Another part of history gone, but replaced with something new. I guess that really does verify the cosmic law that Death gives Rebirth.

So anyway, I would finish my show, then take a few minutes in my dressing room, freshen up and then go out into the lobby. I would be pretty much naked except for a robe or a slip-on and of course a pair of bitchin' heels. In the bright light of the lobby I would sit on the laps of various audience members totally naked except for some heels, and the stagehand would snap a Polaroid of me sitting in a guy's lap. I would sign the Polaroid, give the guy or girl a kiss on the cheek, collect my dollars and move on to the next. Keep in mind the theater held about a hundred people and I did five shows a day, so you do the math. I can assure you it was worth every moment spent sitting on strangers' laps. Sometimes I got lucky and got to sit on a few famous laps. I am not going to kiss and tell, but there were a few actors, athletes and one very hot magician that I had the pleasure of being with after the show and taking a photo. No it isn't an oxymoron, there are hot magicians out there. Often I would get to do a lot more than sit on their laps, at an after-show hook up. I had some incredible sexual encounters with people that I met at Show World. I was a lucky girl.

Once again, I loved to fuck. And of course I still do. The show schedule was a bit grueling actually at five shows a day, but I hung in there to the best of my ability. At the end of the week I was seriously tired and seriously sore and I don't just mean leg and back muscles, my pussy and my throat ached as well. You have no idea how sore you can get until you fuck yourself on stage five times a day, six days a week. Don't believe me? Try it.

After a week at Show World, I needed to take a week off to recuperate making porn movies. The year was 1987, It was still cool to be promiscuous, AIDS was still that that weird cancer that gay men were getting and it didn't really involve any of us other sexually active types. The doctors weren't even sure how AIDS was being transferred and the rest of us were more than happy to continue in our stream of denial that it wasn't going to happen to us. This bubble was going to explode in about a year. I remember even when people first started talking about AIDS. Once a guy said that he wasn't sure he would fuck me because he was worried about AIDS. When I reminded him that we had unprotected sex about six months earlier, so if I had it he did too, we just kind of laughed it off and got down to business.

We all worked hard and played hard; we lived the life of sex, drugs and rock and roll to the max. Another thing that happened when I was in New York, I had the pleasure of meeting Robin Byrd, of *The Robin Byrd Show*. She took over a show that was hosted by Bobby Hollander that was called *The Hot Legs Show*. This was a TV show that was shown in New York City only, it was on the public access channel that came on late at night. The premise of the show was that Robin would have performers come and do a little dance and then she would sit and talk with them after, sort of Johnny Carson style. Robin Byrd is a stunning blonde bombshell, who was always super tan and wore a crocheted bikini on the show. She starred in *Debbie Does Dallas* as Mrs. Hardwick, and in a few other porn movies.

She would have all kinds of performers on the show, straight, gay or trans, it didn't matter; it was an equal opportunity freak show. Even famous people came on the show like Sandra Bernhard. Robin's show was super fun, and was great advertising when you were working at Show World, and a must. I had at least 15 performances on the Robin Byrd show; I did it for a couple of reasons. One, because it was fun. Two, because she became one of my dearest friends to this day. The Byrd, which is what anyone who is really close to her calls her, had a similar childhood to mine; we were both orphaned at an early age with no known brothers or sisters, so we adopted each other as sisters. While there is not any big physical similarities between the two of us—Byrd has brown eyes, I have blue, Byrd has a straight nose, I have a short-turned up nose, etc.—there is a similar energetic appearance. Even to this day when she or I say that we are sisters, people often say, "Oh, yeah, I see the resemblance." She truly was, and still is, New York City's best-kept secret. I love her ten times infinity.

While the building that once housed Show World is still there, the real Show World is long gone. It went under many years ago when Guliani was doing his clean up of Times Square. They passed a law where an adult store needed to have sixty percent non-adult product to sell and forty percent could be adult. We called it the 60/40 law and it killed many an adult bookstore all over the country. Times Square now looks like Disneyland or Las Vegas with all of the neon crap and the chain restaurants. It may be safer, only because it is lit up like an operating room, and more tourist friendly, but part of what New York City was is now gone forever.

7

The next gig I worked was the Mitchell Brothers Theatre in San Francisco. It was a crazy place. Hunter S Thompson once called it the "Carnegie Hall of public sex in America". That's pretty accurate. Hunter could turn a phrase.

I loved the Mitchell brothers. Art and Jim Mitchell were the best. They had created some of the hottest porn in cinema history with some of the hottest porn stars ever such as Marilyn Chambers and they were also responsible for making classic movies such as *Behind the Green Door* and *Insatiable*. I can't tell you how many times I have watched, jerked off to and/or had wild sex with these movies and loved every minute of it. Marilyn Chambers had it all going on; she was beautiful, had a great body, and one could tell beyond a shadow of a doubt that she loved every bit of the sex she had on camera. She was a great image-maker for every porn star of my generation. A funny thing about her that a lot of people don't know is that she was the Ivory Snow girl. Her face graced the box of Ivory Snow holding a baby, until she became the famous porn star and the Ivory Snow people decided to change the box. I mean how could you be a cute mom and a cocksucker at the same time? It just wasn't possible.

I saw Marilyn perform live on stage early on in my career; she did a little dancing, then answered some questions and did a demo of how she could breathe herself to an orgasm. Marilyn had claimed to be studying Tantra and learning spiritual sexual Eros. She laid down on the stage naked and starting breathing, you could visibly see the sexual energy rising up between her legs, through her belly, chest and escaping through her exhale. I almost got off just looking at her. She kept breathing and building the energy up until she finally climaxed, and what a climax it was. I sat watching with my jaw dropped, the only thing I could think at the time was how much I wanted to learn how to do that! And about ten years later I did. If there is another way to get off out there I am going to find it.

There were a lot of other really great image makers as well back in the day, such as Sharon Mitchell, Vanessa Del Rio, Annie Sprinkle, Sharon Kane and many more. These women gave my generation the image of enjoying sex for what it was, a natural, pleasurable act. They were never exploited because they didn't allow themselves to be; they were always in control of their bodies, minds and spirits. They were completely natural in their bodies and their sexual expression. I would like to think that some actresses that came after me thought the same of me.

The Mitchell Brothers Theatre was another place that made me feel like I was home. It was a huge building located in a shady part of San Francisco, the Tenderloin district as a matter of fact. The Tenderloin area of San Francisco has long been known as one of the freakiest parts of one our freakiest cities. Needless to say I adored it.

The whole building where I performed was painted so that visually one had a feeling like he or she had just dropped into a trippy ocean scene, with fish, whales, and sharks, all painted in beautiful realistic colors so it literally looked like the ocean had swept up and gathered you in. It could be seen for quite a ways away and of course everyone who worked there when giving directions always referred to it as the building with all the fish on it. It was a great marketing tool. This place had a similar vibe to Show World minus the circus feel. It was a little more sedated when you walked in, but really what wouldn't be? I imagine Hell would be a tad more sedated than Show World

When one entered there was a foyer inside the door, which had all of Marilyn Chambers' posters up and a greeter who stood behind a glass case where they were selling Marilyn Chambers' movies on VHS. It was twenty bucks just to walk in the door. This kept the creepers out: the guys who came into adult bookstores with their hands in their pockets, looking at the magazines and movie posters while secretly rubbing their cocks in their pockets, thus preventing them from spending any money.

We were here to make money. There are different types in the fetish world; some of them actually enjoy paying. There are all sorts of doms out there who get cash on a regular basis from men who get off on being used financially. Then there are types that understand that to get what they wanted they were going to have to spend some cash. This was the vast majority of the clients that I had. They knew to get what they wanted they were going to have to spend money. Then there were the creepers. They wanted what I was offering but didn't want to pay a cent for it. Obviously this type of client and I did not get along very well.

After a person got through the front foyer there were paths that led to the big theater, which held about three hundred people and to smaller show rooms, like the Copa room. There were also individual peep booths, and video viewing booths. Art and Jim Mitchell were in essence a couple of crazy San Francisco hippies; they had taken the average run-of-the-mill adult bookstore and made it hipper and sexier, and became rich doing so. For instance, in the individual viewing booths they had vibrating metal plates installed on the floors, so when you were watching a movie or a private show with a girl, the floor would vibrate underneath you. In the Copa room, there was a small padded round revolving stage; the room was small and held about 25 people, seated in booths around the stage. The audience members were given flashlights when they entered the show room. As I recall the shows were usually girl-on-girl. When the show began the lights in the room were turned off and the only light in the room was now coming from customers shining their flashlights on the girls as they performed various sex acts with each other.

The guys loved this room; one because it was so small and intimate, and two because of the quirky thing that they got to shine the light on the body parts and sex acts that they wanted to see. I think it brought out the summer camp Peeping Tom in them, and of course because they were all in booths, none of them could see each other. It was fabulous for the customers but just kind of weird for the performers because you could never really see well, you had to feel your way around. We called it the Helen Keller room or the Braille room.

The Mitchell Brothers Theatre was especially known for girl-on-girl shows since all of the girls who worked in the theater were mostly lesbians. Or at least did a damned good job pretending to be.

Hanging out with Art and Jim Mitchell was an experience that is hard to describe. On the one hand they were super fun and totally easy going guys; walking upstairs to their office, one would usually smell the sweet essence of high grade marijuana wafting down the hall, along with loud rock and roll music and laughter. Occasionally, though you would hear them screaming at each other, at the top of their lungs, in a way that sounded kind of scary. I never really knew if the fighting was serious or just some kind of drug induced fit, of course later we learned that they were really fighting to the point of Art threatening to kill Jim and vice-versa. Years later Art did just that. Jim supposedly had been told numerous times to "do something" about his alcoholic and drug-addicted brother. The quick version of the story goes something like this. Art shows up at Jim's house late at night, shouting obscenities and threats towards Jim on the front lawn. Jim is at home with his wife and children. Jim tells Art to go home. Art escalates the situation, firing off a gun. Jim defends himself and his family, and in firing back, hits Art. Art dies. After a long trial Jim goes to jail for many years and dies in prison. It was a shock to the business and to everyone who had ever worked at the Mitchell Brothers. There was no happy ending to this story, only sadness and despair. People will say that "our kind" deserves this or that this kind of thing is bound to happen in the shady business of porn, so we reap what we sow. Well, let me tell you this sort of thing happens everywhere from Politics to Religion to Organized Crime, This, sadly, is how life presents itself to us at times. The only thing we as individuals can do is learn something from the experience. I will also add that empires like the Mitchell Brothers, much like ancient Rome, will always teeter on the brink of destruction. That's what makes it so attractive.

I guess none of us will ever really know if Art was just losing it mentally or if the years of drug and alcohol abuse had finally taken its toll or if on that fatal night Jim really shot in self defense. But the story of Art and Jim Mitchell ended in a sad tragedy, losing two great men that were legends to the porn industry. A few years ago Marilyn Chambers crossed over to the great round as well, so in this way the circle is complete. All three of them were very special to me, and to many others inside and outside the porn biz. May they all rest in peace.

When I performed at the Mitchell Brothers Theatre, it was on the big stage during intermission between the movies that they would show. The stage was high up in the air and the seats were low to the ground so the audience was far away from me, in other words I couldn't reach down and touch them. San Fran was a lot like NYC, when I was at Show World, in regards to the legalities; we were still doing masturbation shows on stage and girl/girl shows. The moneymaking gig here was to get guys to throw money on the stage and then after the show purchase memorabilia from you, such as Polaroids, 8x10 glossy photos, t-shirts, and so forth. Both Show World and The Mitchell Brothers paid the feature acts a very good wage for the week, which usually entailed four to five shows a day Monday through Saturday. Sunday was a travel day where the girl would either be going home or to the next city for the next gig. In the late '80s-to-early

'90s there were only a few porn stars that were touring, which allowed us to keep a good consistent rate per week.

This bubble starting breaking in the mid-'90s for several reasons. First of all, every girl who had ever made a porn movie was immediately hitting the road to dance. They saw the money that we were making and wanted a piece of it. Most of them didn't know how to dance, had minimal costumes, props, etc., and basically couldn't put on a show if their life depended on it. This of course hurt the market; all of a sudden there was bad product out there and over-saturation. Back in the day it was a big deal to see a porn star dance, now every weekend there was a different girl at the local club trying to make a few extra bucks, claiming to be a porn star.

For about eight years, I danced everywhere I could and in all types of places. It was an odd life and it kept me grounded. At times I felt like a big movie star and then there was other times where I would be dancing in this tiny little bar where it seemed like no one knew who I was. I always loved it though.

So many of the clubs had the same sort of rules that we girls had to follow. Often you were only allowed to take off your top and legally had to keep your bottoms on. There were many variations on this depending on where you were in the USA. In some places you could be topless with a thong on, sometimes you could be topless but you had to wear pasties or latex covering your nipples and a thong, other times it was okay to be topless but only with a full bottom bikini on. The whole thing was really quite ridiculous. Protecting grown men from my pussy. Really.

I danced many times in Dallas Texas at a very large, upscale gentleman's club where you could be topless but had to have on full bikini bottoms, the law stated that the dancer must have a least six inches of material covering the buttocks. So not only could you not see my pussy but also be careful if you saw too much of my ass as well. Heaven forbid.

The way the club and law enforcement measured this six inches was with a dollar bill, since paper money is known to be six inches long, it was relatively easy to hold a dollar bill up to the dancers buttocks and see if she indeed had the required amount of cloth covering her buttocks. Now that I think of it someone probably has a fetish of holding up money next to a stripper's ass. You name it and someone is going to get off on it.

Needless to say every girl's ass is a different size so what covered a girl's ass that was 5'3" and weighed 100 lbs was completely different than what covered a girl's ass that was 5'10" and weighed 180 lbs. Guys that liked small tight asses were out of luck, where the dudes that like asses that were big and jiggly were not affected by the 6 inch rule at all. As always the big assed girls have all the luck!

The nipple-covering laws in Texas were similar; the law stated that the nipple and areola needed to be covered. This sounds pretty straightforward but this left a lot of room for interpretation for both the girls and club owners. Some clubs owners insisted that the dancers cover their nipple areas with traditional cloth pasties, some owners allowed the dancers to use a liquid latex to cover the nipples and some owners actually had the dancers cover their nipples with band aids! Again, there is probably some guy out there that gets turned on by the thought of band aids over nipples but believe me the girls did not like it.

Let me tell you none of these choices were really great for the performer, all choices involved glue or tape on a very sensitive area of the body. The traditional pasties had to be glued or double sided taped, the liquid latex had to be painted on at least thirty minutes before your show and it always left your nipples looking like they had some strange mutation going on. Eventually some of the dancers started sprinkling glitter onto the wet liquid latex, to create glitter nipples, which was just as irritating but at least they sparkled. The band aids were a laugh to me; we usually used the round band aids of course, which worked great for me but girls with huge nipples and areolas needed to use the large rectangle band aids which just looked stupid and were irritating as hell to pull off. If you were lucky you could put your pasties, latex or band aids on at the beginning of the day and not have to take them off or reapply them until the end of your shift. Because, hopefully, by that time you would have a good buzz on to dull the pain.

However the reality was a bit different because usually my first show was midday and my last show midnight, which meant a lot of dancing, sweating and clothes going on and off. Usually the need to reapply or change your nipple covering happened at least once or twice in a day; now multiply this by six days for the gig. Needless to say it got old. I hated working in the topless clubs that had these rules. Most of the time the rules revolved around the liquor licenses and whether or not the clubs served booze or not. Because everyone knows that if a man is drinking a scotch or a beer, he could not possibly control himself he if saw a naked nipple. Thank God between my nipples being covered and the lack of booze being served I made it through those days alive and so did the men and women in the clubs. Ha!

The other train of thought was that it was somehow unsanitary; meaning that if there was scotch, beer and or food present with uncovered nipples it would present a health issue. Possibly some fluid from my nipple would drip down into his Pabst Blue Ribbon or on his onion rings. And then of course all hell would break loose. In fact it is possible that the world might even end. I would love to see a *South Park* skit on this topic!

Of course the real game here was that the local governments were desperately trying to stop and control the topless clubs in any way, shape or form that they could They would find any kind of argument to prevent stripping and nudity. The idea was that if they made it as hard as they could for performers and club owners that maybe we all would just stop.

Each city and county had its own set of rules and laws it had to follow; there were usually several pages of rules and laws written down for a dancer to read before each gig. They had laws regarding the type of movement that a dancer could do on stage, which usually fell under the lewd and lascivious type of law, meaning that a dancer could not perform any type of dance that suggested sexual activity in any way. Isn't this how they managed to ban Elvis? I was arrested many times for lewd and lascivious actions. The problem was I never knew what was going to be considered obscene. Was it a simple movement of the hips; was it the floor show where I would literally roll around on the floor, moving myself in every possible position; or was it when I climbed the pole, gyrating myself back down, with the pole between my legs? Was I supposed to stand like a choir boy and, sway back and forth smiling and snapping my fingers while they played "Pour Some Sugar On Me"?

At a certain point I became a rebel, and stopped giving a fuck and just did what I wanted to do. I would often watch club owners having a heart attack at the back while I performed on stage. I was very lucky; any time I was arrested or ticketed for any offenses, the club owners always went to court for me, pleaded my case and paid the fine. The reality of it was that the cops were really just trying to bleed the owners dry so they would shut down.

There was the time in Louisville Kentucky, where I was ticketed for dancing without pubic hair. Yes, believe it or not, in the mid '90s it was illegal to dance naked on stage in Louisville Kentucky with a shaved pussy. I mean, I guess if I had a hairy and unshaved bush that isn't obscene; not even a little. However, the feature entertainer the week previous to me who did an Alice Cooper tribute as well as the Pussy Power show. This is where she would sit naked in a large stage prop that looked like a champagne glass full of water, sucking the water up her vagina and squirting it out like a fire hose. Seriously, how is anyone going to follow that up? I heard the guys on the tip rail had paper cups to try to catch the "water." I also heard that when she was menstruating she would call it "pink champagne." Forget that she also had a coffin with a huge python in it! But none of these acts got her arrested or even ticketed, while my little shaved pussy was obscene; something about portraying child pornography.

The clubs owners started to get around all of the liquor laws by opening up juice bars, meaning a club where the dancer was naked on the stage and was able to do naked lap dances but there was no booze, beer or wine served on the premise; only soda and juice. I thought this was a great idea, no more stupid latex on the nipples or bottoms on. Again they tied all these laws in with booze, so if you were the owner and you cut out the booze then the laws didn't apply anymore.

The down side was that it was always easier to get guys to open their wallets when they had some liquor in them. I mean, let's face it: if a guy has had about six vodka tonics and I am gyrating around in front of him, all of a sudden he doesn't give a fuck that his wife has been sitting at home waiting for him for hours, or that she is going to be pissed, or that right now he is throwing away the rent money because he wants my ass in his face. That same guy stone cold sober is going to be a lot harder to get to drop three hundred bucks, because when sober he is terrified of his wife beating the shit out of him.

With that said the power of pussy was very compelling as well, so it balanced itself out in the end. It is a funny thing the marriage between booze, sex and the lack of impulse control.

I never really fit in as the normal topless gentleman's club girl, the biggest reason being that I choose not to get a boob job, or more politely a breast augmentation. By the '90s, boob jobs were the rage; doctors had finally figured out a way to perform good boob jobs for a reasonable price. Almost every topless dancer, porn star, prostitute and housewife with a few extra grand was getting a boob job. It truly was an amazing thing.

In the business of course a lot of girls got one just out of fear. All of us knew in some way that our careers were short and limited by how preserved we were, and if every other girl had perfect boobs except for one girl whose tits were all floppy and jiggly, then the jiggly girl would probably be lining up for a boob job first thing the next morning. The big secret of course is there are a lot of guys out there that like jiggly, both in ass and in tits, but no one is supposed to know that, I guess. The big secret is that lots of guys actually prefer smaller boobs.

Personally I could never do it because for one thing I hate surgeries and the idea of letting a doctor cut into my chest and stuff a plastic bag full of water into the incision was not going to happen. Let me repeat that. They would knock me out, and as I lay there unconscious and drooling they would cut my tits open with a knife, stuff a plastic bag full of water into my chest then stitch me back up. And I would pay for this. WTF?

The other reason was of course that there was no guarantee if the finished product was worse than what I started with. I had the joy of seeing many boob jobs that looked like Frankenboob. Sometimes they were lopsided or uneven or just hard as a rock; at times it looked like someone had glued plastic forms to their chest. Once I had gone with a girlfriend to be supportive while she got her new titties. The doctor invited me into the surgical viewing room since I was an ex nurse. I was horrified watching the surgery. It was brutal. Yes, I know most surgeries are brutal, but this was scary brutal, mostly because it was elective; meaning it was not necessary for the continuation of life, it was an elective plastic surgery. I decided early on that I would keep the boobs that I had been given and love them as they were, a nice handful with cute pink nipples. Thus it was challenging to compete in the topless clubs with all of the girls who were choosing to get the DDD boobs. They might have the boobs but I had something else. I was Porsche Lynn; I loved myself, loved what I did, and was good at it.

I loved dancing, I loved performing, loved traveling, and loved meeting all of the people that I met. I realized the happiest place for me to perform was in the nude clubs. It is where I started and where I felt the most at home always.

8

The other thing that I started to realize at this time in my life was that money wasn't always the best or most important thing. It wasn't always in my best interest to just do what I could make the most money at and I knew this more every day. In other words, in one's work there comes a time when it is better to choose the job that feeds you in more ways than money, a job that feeds you with happiness, health, harmony, humor, hope; and hopefully if one does this the money would come. Even if it didn't it was still more important to me to be happy.

I was starting to build my character and I was becoming a woman and more of who I am to this day. Porn was starting to build its character too. In 1988, a porn producer named Hal Freeman decided enough was enough. He had been arrested for pandering and hiring someone to have sex for sexual gratification. It was another attempt by the government to monitor and harass the porn industry. In essence they were saying that he was a pimp.

Mr. Freeman took the walk down the plank for the rest of us smut makers, peddlers of flesh, kinksters and perverts. Previously pornographers had been choosing to pay the fine and move on. The fines were usually small and involved minimal jail time. Freeman lost in the lower court in California, but he then arranged to get his case heard before the California Supreme Court. The Court's final decision was that hiring a female or male for the purpose of making a movie, which might include graphic sex but no obscenity was not pandering and therefore legal. Basically they said the only way it wouldn't be legal was if he were paying people to gratify either himself or the actors on set.

It was a happy day for all of us in the San Fernando Valley of California. This meant no more sneaking around to shoot movies, no more leaving LA county to shoot movies and of course there wasn't any reason to go to Europe to shoot movies. This was a definitive moment in time for porn. We were finally getting legitimized.

To add salt to the wound, the prosecution for the case tried to appeal the case to the United States Supreme Court. Justice Sandra Day O'Conner ruled that the decision by the California Supreme Court was constitutional and eventually all of the Supreme Court judges made the same ruling. So, it would stand in California that hiring females and males to act in XXX movies was legal. And so it began, the largest porn boom in history started in the San Fernando Valley. Most everyone was still shooting on VHS and now that they were able to do it legally in the Valley, a constant stream of pornography began flowing. Porn stars were working anywhere from two to six times a week; the money was flowing in like a river. At the time I was still under a contract with Dino Ferrari, but this would be coming to an end by 1989. There simply was no reason to spend the money to send porn stars to Europe.

Also gone were the days of big elaborate productions, as they were no longer needed. For a while, we in the porn business wanted to emulate Hollywood and increase our production values, but at this point most producers came to realize something. People wanted their porn down and dirty: they wanted sex and nothing but the sex. They didn't want dialogue, ornate sets and such; they just wanted to see the dirty deed. Say it was a movie about me and a guy and a girl. We could spend all sorts of time building the plot, and me talking to the guy, and talking to the girl, and we could have costumes, and it could be set in France in the 1920s… or the three of us could just rip off each other's clothes and fuck. It turned out that more people preferred the latter. Porn had gone full circle and back to its roots.

The VCR also brought with it the ability to fast forward through any of the parts of the movie that you didn't want to watch. I must admit that I had burned out many a VCR because of the constant fast forward or rewind. And don't forget the freeze frame where if you like something I am doing you can just make the movie stop and keep me frozen for eternity.

As much as I loved working with Dino Ferrari, I was happy to move on with my career, and going back to being an independent contractor, which meant that I would be able to work with who I wanted, doing the types of scenes that I wanted. The production company that I was contracted to kept me a bit sheltered; they marketed me as an all-American, apple pie porn-type girl; you know, the classy slut. Which was ok, it served me well professionally, but it wasn't really who I was sexually and it wasn't really who I wanted to be on film. I was always the girl that didn't really know that I was going to get fucked so hard and by so many people until it happened, or I was the girl that was curious but had never gone down on another girl before. I wanted to stretch and do different parts.

It was fun being a free agent. I had always loved dark skinned men; as a matter of fact my first boyfriend in kindergarten was black, maybe it was really true once you go black you don't go back. I was really attracted to any nationality that was different than mine, so I had a thing for anyone with skin, hair & eyes darker than mine. Whether it was Blacks, Asians, Mexicans, or Indians, if they were good looking then I was turned on. It was fun to be able to work and let my freak flag fly a little bit more than I used to and play a little more of the top instead of always being the bottom.

The late '80s and early '90s were an exciting time for me. I had complete freedom over my career, I was really comfortable in the sex biz and I was ready to go for it. I got to work with all of the great directors that I had always wanted to work with. Of course a few of them really stand out; Bruce Seven and John Stagliano, just to name two.

Bruce Seven was always a pleasure to work with. He truly loved women and it showed. He treated the girls on set like princesses and in the end got some of the hottest, girl-on-girl scenes that were ever caught on video. Bruce was consistently winning awards through the mid '80s and '90s for Best Girl-on-Girl Movie and the porn stars who starred in his videos were always winning for Best Girl-on-girl Scene. The best thing about working with Bruce is that you knew that you were going to have a relaxed day with some great girl/girl sex, and who wouldn't want that? Well okay, maybe you don't but I sure as hell did!

Being my own boss meant driving to a set located somewhere in the Valley and going to work. I loved being an independent contractor in porn. It meant that I was making all the decisions; not only which movie I was in, but who I wanted to work with, what I wanted to wear and so on. I got to work with everyone that I had always admired. Bruce Seven was one that I choose to work with right away. I had heard all kinds of stories from other girls about working for him. Bruce was known for making all-girl movies, but not just any kind of all-girl movies; the best, raunchiest, hottest, nastiest, sexiest, all-girl movies ever shot. So I guess it goes without saying that I wanted to be in them.

Bruce's movies always won all of the lesbian awards and had the hottest porn stars, doing the nastiest things that you would never see anywhere else. He and his movies were loved by straight guys and lesbians alike; he turned everyone on. People always made comments to him about, "how did you get so and so to do that anal scene, she never does that for anyone else." It was true that Bruce could get porn stars to do the most outrageous sex scenes on and off camera, and he did it in a way that was inviting with absolutely no pressure. I was one of the ones that did things for Bruce that I hadn't done for anyone else.

Bruce had many secret ways about him. First was the fact that he loved women; honestly, he worshipped women and thanked them everyday for their presence in his life. This wasn't fake, he really did. One can tell when someone is faking something like that and Bruce wasn't.

Bruce was a Vietnam Vet and admitted to the fact that it was the presence of the women around him that helped him heal from the war. When you were on a set with him he treated you with complete respect, love, care, and patience. Bruce always had alcohol on his sets, beer, wine, booze; anything you wanted really. I know all the haters are going to say that he was getting the girls drunk and encouraging them to do outrageous sex scenes. Not true, the alcohol was indeed available on the set, but it was never pushed or forced on anyone. Furthermore, most of us were having a drink or two at the most. What's wrong with that? Believe me, if you were getting ready to be fucked up the ass with a huge dildo, you would want a glass of wine first. If you don't believe me I will be right over with a huge dildo and a bottle of vodka and we can run a couple of tests on you.

Bruce also made it ok for us to smoke a little weed on the set, again I refer back to my previous comment. That's all I ever did or saw on the sets. If there were harder drugs, I did not see them present.

When it came to sex Bruce always let us pretty much do what we wanted. He would encourage us at the beginning of the scene, and tell us that he needed some really good nasty stuff from us. He would always have a script so there was always a bit of dialog and he always chose the sets. It was like having a porn cheerleader at the beginning of the scene. He would tell you the things that he wanted to see: "Lots of kissing, pussy licking, lots of finger fucking, some anal finger fucking, a little asshole licking and lets see what kind of dildos we can use. Sound good girls?" Once we started rolling, Bruce would rarely stop the action, which to a porn star is a godsend. Why? Because it keeps the sex rolling and flowing of course.

It cannot be overstated how much of a drag it is to work with a director who is constantly stopping the scene and then starting it over again when you are doing porn. When directors or producers stop the action for long periods of time, it makes the energy between the players stagnant, and makes it very challenging to the male to "keep wood," a term for keeping an erection in porn. Think about it in real life. You and your girl are starting to get it on and the phone rings, or the baby cries, or her husband comes home and all of a sudden your rock-hard cock isn't so hard anymore.

Luckily, in all-girl movies we didn't have the wood issue, although stopping sex scenes for long periods of time once they have started it is not a good idea, even if you are fucking with plastic cocks. Bruce Seven said one of the reasons he only made all-girl movies was that he never had to wait for wood or the money shot. Although this is true, I still think the real reason is because he just loved women and wanted to surround himself with them. I know a few guys that are the same way. I mean if you are a guy and going to be a porn director and you can manage to do a porn movie with all women, wouldn't you?

Since we were now shooting on VHS tape it was wicked cheap and easy to just keep the tape rolling. Bruce may come in here and there and adjust something to get a better shot or suggest another position, but it was always quick. Because of all of these reasons Bruce Seven managed to direct and produce the hottest, all-girl movies in the porn industry for over ten years. He started with Ginger Lynn and his beloved partner Bionca and continued making porn even after he suffered the effects of a stroke, the complications of which eventually killed him.

I have many memorable scenes with Bruce, most of which came later in his career when he turned to making BDSM (Bondage/Discipline Sadism/Masochism) movies. The early Bruce Seven memories are more like *Hard Rockin' Babes*; this was a typical '90s style movie with hot chicks dressed like glam rockers having wild sex. The movie ends with one of Bruce's trademark oil orgies. I had wrestled in mud and Jell-O and was looking forward to the oil thinking it would be a lot less icky. You see, when you wrestle in a substance, whether it be oil, mud or Jell-O, and you are wearing a very small swimsuit, the substance finds its way into every crack and crevice on your body, your armpits, the crack of your ass, pussy lips, even your ears.

When I wrestled in mud took it some scrubbing to get off, it would take some time to get totally clean. The Jell-O kind of melted away but always left a weird sugar coating on your skin that stayed there for quite a while. So my theory was that the oil would be kind of soothing,

I realized that it was going to work its way into every crack, but thought that my body would absorb it and allow my skin to get moisturized. Well, this was somewhat true. The famous orgy scenes were almost always shot on a huge black-out set, meaning all the walls were covered in black duvatine cloth with a huge stage platform in the middle also covered with a piece of black plastic. This gave the illusion that the walls were non-existent, they just sort of faded into the background. These scenes are a pain in the ass to shoot, first of all getting ten female porn stars to be ready to fuck at the same time is a feat in itself.

Think about it: they all have to go through makeup & hair; they all have to douche, smoke that last cigarette and so on. Can you imagine having to get ten chicks all ready to fuck at the same time? That is the funny thing about us girls. To so many guys the thought of having two girlfriends is a dream come true until it actually happens, then the insecurities come out. Well Bruce had to get ten women all worked up, happy and ready to go all at the same time.

When you as the director finally have all ten porn stars on the set ready to shoot, the issue becomes how to keep the camera getting all of the good shots. If you have ten people fucking, one camera can only pick up maybe five people in one shot at a time. Bruce used two and sometimes three or four cameras to shoot these scenes.

My first time working with him I stepped onto the set, just as the production manager was pouring olive oil from huge gallon jugs onto the black plastic covered stage platform. "Oh my God," I thought to myself, "we are going to wrestle and fuck in olive oil," feeling the creepy factor going up my legs. Are you fucking kidding me? On the realistic side, I knew there was nothing wrong, or unhealthy, with the olive oil. Bruce claimed that the olive oil was great for the skin, hair and nails. I can testify that the oil was not the worst. The pit and the stage would always get a little dirt in it, which became like the pea under the mattress. Even though it was small it was noticeable. The oil managed to find itself in every crack and crevice, every one. But somehow through all of this, Bruce Seven managed to crank out some of the hottest, girl-on-girl orgies on film or tape.

Being that this was my first one, I kind of felt like a porno virgin. The scene was fantastic, with a ton of super hot girl-on-girl sex. As great as these scenes were they also produced some of the worst yeast infections ever. Think about ten girls naked on black plastic with olive oil everywhere; dildos, vibrators and fingers going in every hole, mouth, pussy and ass; into every girl and then coming out of that girl and going in another one. The oil traps every thing and the rubber dildos trap everything else. After all the scenes were shot, the toys were basically thrown into a cardboard box until the next shoot. Can you imagine the bacteria that could be cultured with that mess? I can and I did.

It was with Bruce that I was able to truly explore and experiment with my own sexuality. I was now thirty and also super horny. I literally wanted to fuck all the time. Bruce gave me a space to try out a lot of anal play, which I eventually came to really enjoy. He also gave me the space to work with anybody I wanted.

Along with *Hard Rockin' Babes*, another big one that he did was *Where the Girls Sweat*. As I said his movies were notoriously famous for ending with a girl orgy. I think it happened in every single one. The piece of black duvatine (which was a kind of cloth but felt more like strong plastic) was placed on the floor usually with bumper rails around the entire piece, then several gallons of olive oil was poured onto the surface,. To that now add the entire cast of the movie engaging in a girl orgy and you have a typical Bruce Seven movie ending. It did make for a fairly hot visual image, the slick black surface with about eight very tanned and very toned totally hot chicks writhing around, sliding body parts against body parts, fingers and tongues going into all body orifices. It most certainly sold movies and if you were on the set believe me it was a wild ride. Bruce created a niche in the girl-on-girl market. He is much loved and truly missed even today.

As I said the one bad thing about these girl olive oil orgies, as hot as they may sound, was that everything and I do mean everything inside and out was covered in oil… which is not so bad I suppose; at least it's natural, and healthy for the skin. However, on closer inspection your hair was completely soaked in oil, your ears, eyes, nose, throat, pussy and anus were soaked in oil and no matter how long you stood in the shower after the scene was over; no matter what soap you used, it seemed like you could never completely rid yourself of a thin coating of olive oil on your skin. It took weeks to completely remove the oil and there were always moans and groans from all the girls about never doing it again.

I remember saying that I was never, ever going to do a scene like that again in my life. Inevitably, after six to nine months Bruce would call and ask me to partake in another epic girl/girl movie and I would find myself forgetting all about the ramifications of the olive oil pit. And there I would be with some other girl's naked asshole covered in olive oil an inch from my face while I slid all around on my back.

A lot of other producers and directors were jealous of Bruce's ability to get girls to do unimaginable sexual acts for the camera and would often ask him how he managed it. Bruce would just smile and say, "I'm nice to them," which was completely true; he was one of the sweetest, kindest producer-directors in the biz. Of course it didn't hurt that he let us drink wine and smoke pot on the set. Maybe he hypnotized us, I don't know. For many years after Bruce retired due to a serious stroke and since his death, there has been a term coined on porn sets when it comes to girl-on-girl scenes, often you will hear a director tell the girls that he wants a sex scene, Bruce Seven style. Which is a fitting tribute.

9

Besides doing lots of girl-on-girl movies, as I said, I also set out to make interracial movies. I was lucky enough to have some incredible black male porn stars to work with. My all time favorite was Sean Michaels. It sounds like a cliché, but he was tall, dark and handsome, ridiculously so. He was also intelligent, charismatic and a sexual dynamo. He was also delicious. Did I mention he was a sexual dynamo?

It wasn't long after the Rome trip that my contract with Dino Ferrari ended and I went on to be an independent contractor. Times were a-changing. It was 1990; porn was now legal to shoot in Los Angeles, and the San Fernando Valley became the shooting empire of porn. Most every major porn company found itself a large warehouse and began cranking out movies, still in VHS format. This meant no more long trips to Europe to shoot a movie. For once I could choose whom I wanted to work with.

So, I chose Sean Michaels most often, as well as Julian St Jox and Santino Lee, basically all of the black actors. I love black guys and luckily for the most part they love me too. For many years I only fucked black guys on film and in my bed. I hated the way the adult film business treated black talent. The producers and directors loved to put them in movies but would rarely use them on the box cover or give them any accolades at award shows. Since I was relatively famous and could request whomever I wanted to work with I always choose black actors. I call it my black tail years after the "red tails" the black airplane pilots in WWII. My black tail years lasted about six years, the last six years of my career on film.

My black tail years started off camera, ironically enough. I was on a trip to Milan, Italy. I was signing autographs at a convention there. One of the nights, the Italians took me out to the disco, which is where I met a world champion boxer, who changed my life forever. He was sexy, smart, social and great in bed. I thought that I had gone to heaven. I managed to spend every spare minute of my time with him in Italy. I know everyone wants to know who this man is and some people will claim that they already know, but the point of the story is not who he is, the point of the story is what happened. I do not want to write a kiss and tell book. So keep guessing. Ha.

I have been very lucky to have had many great lovers, some of them very famous and others not. I can definitely say that each and every one of my lovers (even the ones that weren't so good and you know who you are. Or maybe you don't!) assisted in a piece of my healing. I say this because I had somehow built a belief system around the fact that I was not attractive, that I was actually very ugly, that if I was going to find a man, it would be from being smart or having a good personality. This of course is not uncommon with women, even those who are getting a lot of signs from men that they are attractive.

I really thought that I would never get married. I prepared myself to have a job that I could take care of myself. Not really a bad plan when it comes down to it. Through my lovers' reflection I was able to see the real me. Each kiss, each hug, each orgasm helped to heal another piece of me. I have a ton of gratitude to my lovers for the transference of healing energy that was always present, whether they were aware of it or not. In my spiritual path we call this the healing of the genital sense of self. What a great thing to move forward with in life.

I immediately connected with Sean on many levels. I specifically requested to work with him in many films and even shot probably the best sex scene ever with him in the privacy of my own bedroom with the addition of two cameras, a boom guy, and a lighting guy. The scene was for Moonlight Entertainment, a company run by a great group of guys from the East Coast that were on the cutting edge of producing gonzo videos. Basically these guys would make porn videos, shot without any real script, shot on inexpensive sets, that were down and dirty, nothing but sex. Gonzo style was sort of like you were there in the room with the actors. It was very chaotic as opposed to a stylized piece of film.

It was a great concept, quite similar to the old Swedish Erotica movies; there was no script, all sex, and the style on the old Swedish movie was called "loops." The video I shot with Sean Michaels was called *Radical Affairs Number 6* and features a photo of me with over-processed bleach blonde hair wearing a black thong, with a black Louisville slugger baseball bat acquired from a fairly famous black baseball player that I was fucking at the time. I made a vow to myself that this book would not be a compilation of all of the famous athletes and actors, etc., that I fucked back in the day. So, I will not reveal names; one, because I think it is just tacky, and two, because it was a long time ago and sometimes things deserve to be left in the past. The only people I am mentioning in this book are people that worked with me on screen in movies, which is pretty much common knowledge.

I will say that I had the pleasure of fucking a lot of very hot men. Hopefully they remember who they are. It would be quite a shame otherwise. I remember all of them. I went mostly for athletes, because I adore tall, muscular men with athletic ability. I grew up an athlete and was playing sports through high school and college; playing basketball, volleyball and softball, and I ran track. I am a tomboy at heart and have always had an honest connection with athletes; we could always talk sports and then fuck like animals. Or fuck like animals and not talk about sports. Either way. I was a big fan of professional sports. I was attracted to athletes for their well-conditioned bodies, their sexual prowess and strength.

I have great memories of almost all of my lovers, even the one night stands and I am grateful for those memories. I will say it again, I truly love to fuck. I think it is odd that in today's society a woman who is obsessed with status, or clothing, or money is considered somewhat normal while a woman that loves to fuck is considered odd. As much as things have changed over the years some things still stay the same.

Anyway did I mention how much I liked to fuck Sean Michaels? He was a huge sports fan as well, so we often talked sports; we were just like a couple of guys when we were on the set. Sean Micheals was everything that I could ever have wanted in a man, which is how and why I fell hard for him. He remains the only porn star that I ever fell in love with. I had often heard other porn stars talk about the fact that everyone fell in love with someone on a set at least once in their career. Before Sean I found this hard to believe. Mostly because to me having sex in porn was very straightforward: two people or more brought together to accomplish a common goal. It was business, and of course for me it was pleasure, but it certainly wasn't romantic.

While over the years I became very close friends with other porn stars, both female and male, I really could not imagine falling in love with one of them until it happened to me. It took me by surprise, all of a sudden I couldn't stop thinking about him. I requested to work with Sean as much as possible on as many movies as I could. As it was happening, even as a famous porn star I felt the same as anyone would have when they were first falling for someone. Was I being stupid? Did he feel that way about me too?

It was when he introduced me to his girlfriend that I realized how close I had grown to him. When he introduced her to me as his girlfriend, I felt a complete loss of breath, like I had been punched in the stomach. I really couldn't speak, except to whimper, "Nice to meet you." It was like I was back in junior high.

I must have cried a river of tears over this man. I hated being that girl. Here I was Porsche Lynn, the big porn star. All over the world dudes whacked off thinking about me, and here I was following Sean around like a puppy dog. I was thinking about love while he was banging me, while he was probably just spacing out, trying not to blow his load too soon.

I think it was harder because for a while I just didn't realize how I felt about him; the saying that you don't know what you have until you lose it certainly holds true in this case. The awkwardness of falling in love with your leading man just makes one feel oh so high school. Okay, so I had my one time of feeling like a silly girl. I was going to make certain that this was the only time this happened to me. This was a very raw wound for many years because I felt fucked over, but the truth is and was, "He really just wasn't that into me." Plain and simple but why is that so hard for the ego to accept? . The other truth was that I had been on the other side of this equation many times as well, so what goes around comes around; it's universal law. So many times I could sense it when some guy who was fresh to the business would bang me for the first time, then he would be calling me for a week after. This time it was my turn.

The good part of this story is that Sean Micheals and I made some outrageously good porn together and managed to break down a lot of racial and color barriers in the porn biz. The current porn stars can thank us as well as many others for tearing down the racial walls of porn. People like Angel Kelly, Julian St Jox, Santino Lee, and many others made it possible for them to enjoy no color lines. Again, it sounds ridiculous that just thirty years ago it was taboo for a black guy to fuck a white girl on camera but that's the way it was.

I really started accepting roles based solely on who I was going to work with and for. Money was secondary to my happiness and I had complete freedom to do what I wanted with my career. If I didn't like the people making the movie or the people that I was going to fuck, I passed on the movie. This allowed me to make the jump to making porn because I really liked it, not because I needed the money. Working for this reason was completely liberating and the ultimate freedom. I did what I wanted to do when I wanted to do it. I didn't have an agent any more; I was booking myself for movies as well as feature dance gigs. People were making the calls to me, I didn't need to hustle the work, and I didn't need an agent to hustle it for me. It was now 1992. I had about four hundred porn titles to my name and I was famous. Some of the most memorable movies I made at this point were *Night Trips, Arabian Nights, Bend Over Babes* and *Buttwoman*. That's right, I said *Buttwoman*.

Night Trips I recall in large part because it was shot on 35mm film by a director named Andrew Blake. Blake's films are characterized by high production values, artistic stylization, and rigorous technique. He was a true director and had made his fortune and fame with *Playboy* and specifically with the Playboy Channel. His transition to porn was thought of as kind of strange in the day because usually people were constantly trying to transition *out* of porn and go to more legitimate things like *Playboy*. I don't know that I ever really knew the real reason he transitioned to porn, but I will say this: I am glad he did, and so are about ten billion other people. Andrew has come to be one of the most respected porn directors, producers and cameramen in the history of porn. He was the first, and I think the only porn director to ever win an award at a mainstream film festival.

There was a lot of talk about this movie. The word was that the respected movie company Caballero was going to do something amazing with this *Playboy* guy on film. There were several casting calls for it and everyone seemed interested in getting a part. I know what you may think about porn casting calls but I can assure you they are actually some of the tamest casting calls I have been to. There aren't blow jobs involved and no, when the director is done, he doesn't pat you on the ass and tell you to ride his pony.

A porn casting call basically consists of meeting the director and producer, getting naked, having them snap a few quick pictures of you, usually not even showing pink, then you discuss what you do and don't do on camera, and that's it. The do's and the don'ts can get interesting on occasion.

I showed up for the casting call and was auditioning for the female lead. In my view, Andrew Blake looked very unimpressed by what I had to offer although he assured me he would call me if he had a part for me.

I left pretty sure that I was not going to get a part in the movie. I was bummed out but life goes on. I found out a few days later that he had cast the female lead to Tori Welles, who was a gorgeous new porn star; she was a beautiful brunette, with a incredible body. I had to agree that it made complete sense. Tori was new and young, fresh and drop-dead gorgeous. I think she had only done two movies before *Night Trips*. The male lead was cast to Randy Spears, another young, fresh handsome actor who had transitioned from soap operas into porn. Randy ended up having a long career in adult movies.

The leads as far as anyone knew were cast, but there were still a lot of parts left, which I was still vying for; this movie had a major pre-production buzz going on and I wanted to be a part of it. I got a call from the production manager, who stated that there was a part that no one was really interested in, it was the part of the Doctor who is helping Tori with some strange dreams that are taking over her life. The part required the actress to be incognito for most of the movie, since the doctor morphed in and out of the dream scenarios. She would be presented as a classic straight-laced medical doctor with hair in pulled back in bun, wearing glasses and a lab coat. The character would then morph into a strange nymph wearing a silver white wig, some big jewelry, a silk scarf and not much else while engaging in a three way girl-on-girl scene with Tori Welles and Jamie Summers. The next morph for the doctor would be dressed in black leather wearing a white phantom of the opera mask and fucking the male doctor while Tori watched and eventually joined in.

I was into it, it was perfect for me; I loved the idea of being incognito and I was going to have sex with some hot people. What could be better? I did get hired for the part and I will always have immense gratitude to Andrew Blake for letting me be a part of his movies. I got to be a part of the epic porn film, *Night Trips* and working with Andrew Blake was a complete pleasure, and he was extremely professional, mild-mannered and respectful. You could tell that he was seeing the film in his imagination; that he had it painted somewhere in his mind and was now painting it onto the film. He was a consummate artist. There were times when the talent wasn't sure where he was going, but we somehow had faith that he was guiding us into creating beauty, and he was.

Shooting on film is an arduous process of lighting, measuring, re-lighting, then shooting a few feet of film, stopping, readjusting, shooting a few feet of film, stopping readjusting. Shooting on film is very expensive; the cost is per foot or maybe even per inch, so every shot has to count.

Gone was the video mentality of just let the cameras run because tape is cheap. Every scene needed to be set up, the action blocked out and rehearsed, as much as you can possibly rehearse a sex scene anyway. A big part of sex scenes for me had to do with the fact that I was into them of course. It's hard to rehearse sucking a cock. Try it sometime.

At the time of shooting *Night Trips*, it seemed often to those of us on set that Andrew was shooting a bunch of disjointed clips that made no sense as a whole and most of us wondered how he was ever going to glue this stuff together to create a film. Well, he did and then some. There was a proper theatrical release for *Night Trips*, with red carpet media from all sorts of outlets; Caballero did an excellent marketing job for the film. Watching this beautiful film on a large screen was a moment I will remember all my life. Blake had created a masterpiece, he had managed to edit together all bits and pieces into an awesome film. Everyone loved it; the critics raved and *Night Trips* was on its way to becoming one of the classic films of all times. It is a "must have" for all porn aficionados.

Phallix Glass Toys are amazing.

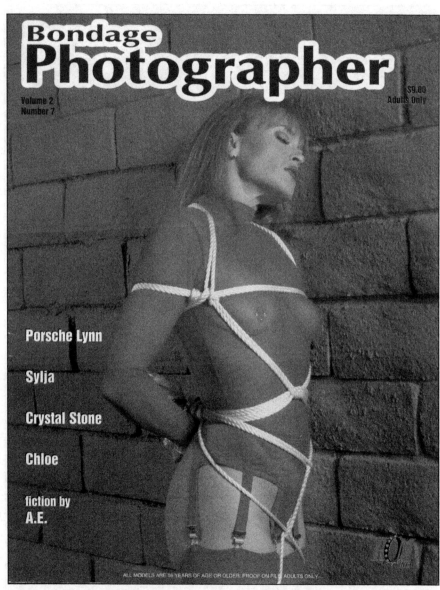

Bondage model, indeed, 1991.

Corset by Stormy Leather, heels by Demask and Firearm by Kimber.

Infamous booty shot.

Getting ready for the next show at Industrial Strip, Gary Indiana.

Glam Shot with Tara Indiana, NYC, 1996.

Me at a Sweet Medicine Sundance, going to the Tree of Life.

Dancing at Sundance, whistles and plumes up!

Riding a blow up, you know what.

Big hair days, early '90s.

Every woman needs at least one red dress.

Legends of Erotica, Las Vegas.

Early Mistress days, 1993.

Fabulicious Nina Hartley.

Original Pink Ladies, Jeanna Fine, NIna Hartley, Angel Kelly and me.

Infamous Porsche Pose, 1992.

John Stagliano, a wonderful leading man.

My Dr. Shivago dress by Religious Sex.

Casual party in my home town Scottsdale, Arizona.

Salute and gratitude for our military. *Hoo-Rah!*

Robin Byrd, Vegas, 1992.

Angel Kelly & me at CES/AVN, Vegas.

Photo taken in the Dungeon Bedroom, DOINYC, 1996.

Photo Credit: Suze Randall- Infamous shot from *The Big Thrill*.
Suze Randall is every Porn Star's bestie!

Photo Credit: Misa Martin, Dress by Trashy Lingerie.

Photo Credit: Misa Martin.

Early Domina days, first nipple piercing, way before it was cool.

Early Domina days, 1996.

Shot in Ernest Greene's dungeon LA.

Tarting around, late '90s.

The Red Years, because I dyed my hair red for a couple of years.

With Robin Byrd after winning Best Actress.

With Penn at AVN.

With Santino Lee at AVN after party.

Amber Lynn and me,
AVN Award show.

Casual moment in a
black leather mini.

Porsche-Lynn – The Look
Photo Credit: Steven Goldstein,
Keyhole Productions

With my Beloved, Angus.

10

So of course I have told a lot of fun stories, and of course I want my book to be fun, mostly because that is what the majority of my time was in the business. I had fun and when I think back on my life and what I have done I would take none of it back. With that said, things were not always sugar and spice and everything nice; there were a lot of challenging times along the way. Besides the time when Mike accidentally hit me with a lamp, there was another incident that gave me a wake-up call. A very scary one indeed.

I was dancing at a strip club called Omar's located in Lansing Michigan very close to the Capitol. It was a great tittie bar; booze and titties were the whole thing there. At the end of the world if a man still had Omar's his world would still be somewhat okay.

The dancers were topless, we all wore thongs with the nude type pantyhose under the thongs but we did not have to wear pasties on our nipples. A strong but gentle Greek man who treated all of us very fairly owned the place. It was the place where I acquired a taste for ouzo, a Greek liquor that tastes like black jelly beans. Oh My God! I love black licorice and I love ouzo too. Omar's was one of the hottest clubs in town; everybody went there from all over the area. It was a constant party. One night I was dancing and I had been alone for a little while so I picked up a really hot guy. He was a bodybuilder, 6'6" tall and totally buff. Yes, it's true: dancers do pick up customers and fuck them, despite what people say.

I know so many guys that have been given shit by their friends for waiting for a stripper. Quite often when the pick up happens, all the guy's friends have left because they think he is a total idiot for trying to pick a

113

girl up. Of course, with that said, most guys who think a dancer is into them are sadly mistaken and go home with their dick in their hands. But again, this does not mean that it is never true. A girl wants what a girl wants, and sometimes it is there right at the club where she is stripping.

I arranged to meet this guy at a hotel because for the most part I didn't really want him knowing where I lived and I didn't trust him enough to go to his place, and getting a cheap hotel to fuck in always seemed like an easy solution. We met at the hotel, had a few more drinks; as I recall we probably smoked a joint and started to fuck. The fucking was going pretty good; I was into it and had several orgasms but the guy just wasn't getting off and was even having a hard time staying hard. I tried everything that I knew: I sucked his cock until my jaw ached, I talked dirty in every language that I knew, I licked his balls for a while but nothing was getting his dick hard. I finally gave up and suggested that maybe "tonight wasn't the night for him." I got up and started to dress, saying that I was going to go home. I wasn't being a dick about it, I just couldn't suck him off anymore and he was too limp to fuck at this point, so what was a girl to do?

He freaked out and basically turned into the Incredible Hulk, except he wasn't green. He literally went on a rage in the room. He started throwing things, and yelling and screaming at me. I tried to chill him out but it wasn't helping; he shoved me around, pushed me down on the bed and was trying to prevent me from getting dressed. This was the definition of bad scene at this point. I finally managed to dress and went to open the door. He shoved the door shut and somehow managed to break the latch of the deadbolt off, making it impossible to open the door. This is when I knew I had a serious problem. Luckily the room was on ground level. I suspected that the screaming and yelling of our voices might be disturbing someone and that possibly the cops were on their way. I went to use the phone to call my roommate, but when I grabbed it "Hulk Boy" pulled the phone cord out of the wall. Remember this was 'way before cell phones. All the guy kept saying was that I wasn't going anywhere.

At this point I had to laugh, I mean I was going to stay there until he came? Come on. I think the romance was over at that point. It was then that he slugged me. I remember feeling completely shocked; the pain was extreme but it was bearable. At that point I had the feeling like I had to get out of that room no matter what. It was either him or me at that point.

I looked around the room trying to think, trying to find something to use back on him. I picked up the phone and hit him with it. I swung it at him with all my might and it connected to his head. This was a bad mistake; it didn't affect him at all. He grabbed the phone cord and wrapped it around my neck and started choking me. I knew that time was running out, I could feel myself starting to black out. I had to do something now, I managed to get my hands between his legs and grabbed and yanked his cock and balls as hard as I could, and he screamed and let go of the cord.

I was done playing around at this point. I grabbed a chair and threw it through the plate glass window. I jumped through it and found the hotel manager standing on the other side. He looked kind of shocked then immediately started giving me shit. The hotel manager was just standing there screaming and yelling at me for damaging his property. I told him that there was a guy in the room that was trying to kill me and he needed to call the police. The police were called, charges were pressed and that was that. I never saw the guy again. But it was a great life lesson.

This is the reason a lot of people are afraid to be who they are and to let their true self out in the universe. Fear. That is why so many women don't go to motels with strange men, because they are afraid of being hurt. Like after that I was supposed to never do something like that again. Fuck that. I liked doing things like that. Not only that but in my whole life this was the only guy who ever did anything like that to me. I wasn't going to let this asshole stop me from enjoying myself and being who I was.

I knew beyond a shadow of a doubt that I needed to get into some kind of martial arts class. I realized that I knew nothing about defending myself. I knew that I was prone to putting myself in dangerous positions and that I had better learn to defend myself or I was going to have a short lifespan. And that was it. I never thought about not putting myself in that sort of position again. That is who I was.

I started studying karate. It was heaven for me: it calmed my emotions, strengthened my physical self and gave me an all-around sense of peace. I loved it. I still study in a dojo today and it still gives me the same feeling. When I walk into the dojo, I feel like I am home and that I am at a place of peace.

Thank God, since the day that I was attacked I have never had to use my martial arts to defend myself. It's a funny thing that happens once you start learning to defend yourself you find that you don't need it anymore. Maybe I was smart enough that I didn't get in fights anymore, or maybe I carried myself a little differently and that people just didn't think about attacking me anymore.

I have only had two other incidents of aggression in the entire time since then. One was in a very crowded strip club, where a guy attempted to grab my wrist. I managed to easily break the wrist lock that he had on me and stomped on his foot. The bouncer interceded and removed the guy from the club and that was that.

The other time was in Philadelphia where I was working at a club called Charlie's Dream, which was located in a bit of a rough area. I had rented a car and was driving myself from the hotel to the club. The hotel was also located in a rough part of town, right next to the city projects.

I was driving back to the hotel very late, about two in the morning. I wanted to get something to eat and a soda, and the only thing open at that hour was the 7-11 across the street. I pulled in, parked the car and got out. I was carrying my handbag on my shoulder with all of my money, credit cards, and my cell phone. I walked into the store, bought some chips and soda, and a few other things, which in total amounted to two bags of stuff. I walked out of the store, and started to go back towards my car. I had my handbag on my shoulder, and was carrying the two plastic bags in my hands. As I walked back to the car, I saw two teenagers walking towards me with their hands tucked into their jackets, like they were carrying weapons. Now people might wonder how I knew, or maybe I was just imagining things. If you think that, then you have never been in that situation. If it's two AM and two dudes are walking towards you like these guys were walking towards me you know that some bad things are about to happen.

Immediately the hair on the back of my neck stood up. I went into a hyper response of sorts. All of my training started to kick in and it felt like time was moving in slow motion, I assessed the fact that they probably had weapons on them, and that there were two of them and one of me. I dropped the plastic bags. I was planning to give up the handbag because I figured that my life was worth more to me that the handbag. By now they were close enough to touch me, I turned to the guy on my right and as soon as I did the guy on my left grabbed my bag. I still didn't see any weapons but didn't know for sure if they were carrying or not. They were both to close for me to kick, I looked around and the parking lot was deserted. The thought of screaming didn't even cross my mind. Once the guy on my left had managed to get the bag he started running back across the street with the other guy in tow. I ran after them, almost catching up with one of them. I don't know what came over me. I was just so fucking pissed off that they were stealing my hard earned money from me. Who did they think they were?

I saw that they were running into the projects a lot faster than I could go. I also knew that even if I caught them, a white girl running into the projects of Philadelphia late at night was not a good idea. So I turned and went back to the store and to my car. The store manager ran out; he told me that he had already called the police because he had seen everything. Okay, well I guess that was better than doing nothing at all. The police pulled into the lot a moment later, I jumped into the back of the police car telling the officers that we could still catch them if we drove quickly over to the projects. For some reason instead of telling me to get out of the car the officer cruised right into the projects with me in the back seat. What the hell was I thinking, right?

I gave the officers a very good description and a very good sense of where they had ran. Believe it or not, we found them sitting on a porch. They didn't look too happy when I jumped out of the back of the police car. The police had called for back up so now there were several other police cars driving around. Not a good scene in the hood. The police managed to shake down the two guys who ended up being just a couple of kids: one 17 and one 18. I almost felt bad; almost, but not really. The cops came over to me saying that they had a certain unlikely amount of cash in the pockets and asking me if I could give them the amount of cash in my purse. As luck would have it, I always counted my cash before I left the club, so I knew pretty much to the dollar how much money I had: $675.00. Seriously, what a couple of dumb-asses these guys were. They steal almost 700 bucks from me and then they just chill out on a porch in plain view waiting to get arrested.

The cops confirmed that it was my cash; also one of them had my cell phone in his pocket. I asked them about my purse, where it was, as I wanted my credit cards, wallet, all of that. As we were talking a couple more cops came up with my purse and a bunch of my stuff. Great, all's well that ends well. I just had to go to the police office in the morning to file a report. Hats off to the Philadelphia Police Department; they did great work and the guys that helped me that night were great people.

I also want to take some time to acknowledge some of the people that I knew and that I lost over the years. For whatever reason, my time in porn was a time when several stars committed suicide. The first in my era that I knew of was Megan Leigh. She was very sweet and beautiful with the girl-next-door look; she came into porn from working with the Mitchell Brothers, where she danced and worked as a house girl. Although deep throat guys in movies knew Megan for her ability, to her friends Megan was always a bit quiet and shy. She became best friends with one of my good friends, Brit Morgan. There were a group of us that hung out together; we even created a social club called the Pink Ladies. Pink Ladies were meant to be a support group for female porn stars.

I remember to this very day exactly where I was when I heard that Megan had shot herself. I had just finished my noon show at Show World in New York City. One of the people that worked there as a helper came into my dressing room to tell me that Megan had shot herself and then thankfully Robin Byrd was there to come to my emotional rescue. I didn't cry at first; I was in complete shock. Somehow, my mind could not wrap itself around the idea and concept that one of my good friends had taken a gun, put the barrel in her mouth and pulled the trigger. And of all people to do this, Megan was probably the last person I could imagine doing so. I could have believed this about a lot of other friends that I had, but not Megan; there was no way that this made sense to me.

The shock actually lasted for several hours. I went about my routine at Show World with lots of people giving me their condolences. After the shock wore off, I had to know the details. I was able to get on the phone with Brit Morgan and her husband who were very close to Megan at the time. They were both just as shocked as I was; they knew that she was going through some problems but had no idea that they were of this magnitude. I had to know more details about what happened. Was she drunk; was she high? Who's gun was it? Where did she do it and who found her? It seemed like the only way for me to put my psyche at ease was to have the details of the picture.

I found out that they were going to do an autopsy. the gun used was Megan's .38 revolver, and she was home with her mother who had found her. There were a lot of things being said about her mother denouncing her lifestyle and not being happy with her choices. The more details I learned the harder it became to swallow. Megan's mother was a registered nurse. The bullet went through Megan's mouth and exited behind her ear, leaving relatively little damage however what I was told was that her mother began chest massage and resuscitation when she found her and pushed the internal blood into her lungs which essentially drowned Megan in her own blood. What the fuck!

We learned that there were only trace amounts of alcohol and valium in Megan's blood, which meant that she was sober when she pulled the trigger. The facts just didn't add up, and the more I learned, the more tormented I became. I hated that Megan was sober, and hated the fact that her mother actually killed her. I hated the fact I felt so helpless. I hate to admit it but I also hated that I had felt like doing the same thing many times but never had the courage to do it. At the end of the day, the only solace that I could find was to honor Megan's choice to do what she wanted with her life. When it is all said and done the greatest gift the Great Spirit gave us is the gift of free will. Each one of us has the final decision on whether to live or die. I truly believe that.

After Megan died, there were about three more suicides; each one produced the same reaction in me as the first. Alex Jordan hung herself from a bar in her closet. It was reported that she did this while her husband was away trying to set up a ski shop so they could leave the business. Her suicide note was addressed to her pet bird.

Another of my friends that I lost at the time was Cal Jammer. He shot himself in his ex-wife's driveway. There were rumors about financial issues and his wife leaving him for infidelity.

My friend and one of my favorite actresses of all time, Savannah, also shot herself. These all happened within a three-year period. The one that got the most media attention was Savannah. I'm not really sure why this was; maybe because she had dated a bunch of famous musicians or just that she was so fucking beautiful that she literally looked like an angel. When I say famous musicians I do mean that they were famous. She dated Axl Rose, Gregg Allman and Billy Idol just to name a few. What I can say is that she was a tortured soul. My heart wept for her.

She never found peace and was always looking for love in all the wrong places. I heard that she shot herself after she ran her car into a fence, which broke her nose and left severe lacerations on her face. She called a friend and said she would need plastic surgery and then she shot herself, in theory because she could not deal with what happened to her face. Although I will never know the reasons how or why she died for certain, I will say that her death made me look at my own mortality, my own unwillingness to live life to the fullest and my own need to heal some deep wounds.

After Megan died, I got clean and sober: no more drugs and no alcohol. The epiphany for me was that I loved to do the alcohol and drugs to take the pain away and it worked. While I was fucked up, pain in every form, whether it was emotional, physical, mental, spiritual or sexual, was gone. But when I woke up the next morning sober, the pain came right back. It not only came back but I felt like shit, too. I hated that.

I began to understand that I didn't even enjoy it, it was just that I was drunk or I was high and out of control. I realized that the only way I was going to get rid of the pain was by doing some work internally on my issues. The drugs and alcohol were just a hamster wheel going around and around that I was running on constantly, giving me a temporary solution to my problems. I also knew that if I didn't do something I would end up like so many of my other friends with a bullet to my head, and deep down inside I really did want to live. My philosophy was that I was going to die eventually anyways, so wasn't it worth sticking around to see how it ended up? My solace was that I knew that some day I would be free of this physical body and all the pain that it had collected over the years, so why not stick around and see how it all turned out. Don't get me wrong: I am mostly a happy person but like a lot of us I struggle at times, and the drugs and booze were just a mask for me to wear, a place for me to hide.

As time goes by some of my most loved leading men have crossed over such as Jamie Gillis and John Leslie, along with one of my favorite directors, Fred Lincoln. Jamie Gillis was always one of my favorite leading men. He was a great fuck on and off camera. He was openly bisexual and also was known as a good director in the business. He had a charismatic presence that was so strong, you could feel him the minute he walked into the room. He could be an extremely dominant alpha male who would take you, own you and eat you alive. Then he would turn into the most submissive little pig, begging to lick your asshole. He was quite a wild ride.

When I think of Jamie Gillis two stories stand out. The first that comes to mind is when we were in a movie together called *Ten Little Maidens*. I was essentially an extra on a porno set; it was early on in my career. The scene called for a couple of serving maids for a large dinner table party. The two serving girls were comprised of myself as well as Nina Hartley. Nina is amazing, by the way. She is still active in the business well into her fifties. The scene was being shot in a really ornate room with a table large enough to sit about ten people around it. All the famous stars were there: Jamie Gillis, Amber Lynn, Ginger Lynn, Tom Byron and so on. The table was decorated with extremely ornate settings and all kinds of food: a suckling pig, vegetables, fruit, potatoes, glasses of wine, and pretty much anything one could imagine.

The gig was that the serving girls were bringing in food and serving people until they became so overcome with lust that an orgy broke out. Typical porno scene, you know? Everyone is just having a nice dinner and then all of a sudden everyone is fucking on the table. Just like in real life. The actors started eating the food and then of course started fucking. They started fucking on the table and then started incorporating the food into the sex. I was standing off camera watching from the sidelines. Jamie was fucking Amber and they were really going at it. I could see him pick up the head from the suckling pig and place it on top of Amber's pubic mound, so it kind of looked like he was fucking the pigs head. Then I looked to his left and there was Tom Byron sliding a carrot into Ginger's asshole and a cucumber into her pussy. This was like only the second porno set that I had ever been on, so I was kind of surprised, but I also thought it was kind of hot.

At some point I walked off the set to take off my wardrobe and get a shower, because essentially I was done with my part of the scene. As I was leaving the shower area, Amber and Ginger were coming in. They were both screaming and yelling at each other. I overheard Ginger telling Amber how gross and disgusting she was, to let Jamie put that pig's head on her. Amber shouted back at Ginger, "Oh yeah? I wasn't the one with a carrot in my pussy and a cucumber up my ass, you stupid bitch!" I was laughing so hard inside that I felt like I was going to die.

I had a sex scene with Jamie many years later. I was fussing around beforehand and complaining to him about the fact that the makeup artists put cocksucker red lipstick on your lips and then you end up with it smeared all over your face, looking like shit. Jamie, said, "Oh, no baby, you don't look like shit. You look beautiful. You look like a hot little pig." I melted. I think I melted the most because of the fact that I got turned on by being told I looked like a little pig. He had a way of worshipping women. He sincerely treated them like goddesses. I mean, who else could tell me I looked like a hot little pig and make me wet but him?

The other Jamie Gillis story: it was common knowledge on all sets that you had to hide your shoes from Jamie, because if you didn't he would get your high heels, sniff them and jack off, sometimes on them and sometimes in them. Jamie came to visit me once in San Francisco while I was dancing at the club. I caught him in my dressing room, in my shoe closet, naked, jacking off with all of my shoes around him. He was so happy, he looked like a kid at Disneyland. Jamie had somehow bribed the manager to let him in. I was so pissed that he was jacking off in my shoe closet, I started beating him with one of the shoes, which of course only got him more turned on. You just couldn't win when it came to Jamie.

John Leslie was another story. I had fallen in lust with John Leslie when I was about twenty years old when I was a young college student having my first real orgasms. Way back when I was at Cinema X, I used to watch him on screen and get turned on. John was the epitome of tall, dark and handsome; God, I fucking loved him. He was Italian and was a total alpha-take-charge-throw-you-down-rip-your-clothes-off-and-fuck-your-brains-out male. The first time I met him was on a movie called *'Porsche Lynn the Call Girl'*. John was to be my leading man. I was totally intimidated by him to the point where I could barely talk to him. John came to me before our scene was about to start and asked me if I would be willing to spend some time with him privately. Oh My God, really? ! Yes, of course I would! We found a private room and began to make out. I started kissing him for real, with no pretense, straight up making out, heavy petting above and below the waist. I was kissing him deeply, my pussy was so wet that I was soaking my panties. John started licking my pussy and I swung my body across his in the classic 69 position so that I could suck his cock at the same time. I love sucking cock; it's still one of my favorite things to do. With John's face buried in my pussy and his cock buried in my mouth, he came in my mouth. What the fuck? He came just minutes before our scene was due to be shot. So basically we snuck off and fucked ten minutes before we were going to get paid to fuck. Not the smartest thing to do on a porn set.

He was freaking out a bit saying that he couldn't believe that he had cum. He told me that it never happened like that and that it usually took hours for him to get off. I asked him if it was going to be a problem to get his dick hard and cum again in the scene and he said he didn't know. Uhmmm. Well, the scene did get shot, it was a totally hot sex scene but no cum shot. We did an internal cum shot, in other words he pretended to cum inside of me, which is very rare in porn, but then again so was John Leslie.

11

When I talk to people about my work in the business the question always comes up about being exploited, and if I was used as a sex symbol and basically treated like a piece of meat. I can honestly say that in years of making porn and the other ten years of doing various adult related activities, I have never felt like either I have always said that I was the one who was exploiting the male sex drive to make money; the one taking advantage of the male's desires and imagination to profit from it. The reality is I feel there is an equal energy exchange. As porn stars, we would give a certain amount of energy to make a scene happen and the energy exchange would be money.

I feel the exploitation stigma is just another way to make women feel badly about being sexual human beings. After all, the religious rules and laws run deeply in our sexuality; the sexual rights and wrongs, do's and don'ts, are based largely on religious beliefs. These beliefs have sculpted us since we were very young, even if we personally didn't come from a religious family. Think about who is really in control? The person who is performing for the money or the person who is paying it? I think that is pretty easy to figure out. I once had a boyfriend who was dominant; he would never, ever be caught dead in a strip club, nor was he into porn. He would get women to do what he wanted through his own power, not through the fact that he had a dollar in his hand. When I was performing, whether in a club or on film, I always felt in control. If a guy didn't know that then I was doing my job even better than I thought.

I never felt like a piece of meat because I have always had a strong sense of self worth, and self love. I have always known that I had value. As far as being a sex symbol, I am flattered. Growing up I adored and worshipped Marilyn Monroe and Elvis Presley. In my opinion they are two of the most iconic sex symbols in our history. After all, what is a sex symbol? If we break down the two words, "symbol" is something that "stands for" or "reminds" us of something else; and then add "sex" to create something that "stands for" or "reminds" us of sex. Yes. I love it. That is me described to perfection. Hopefully I remind you of really good juicy sex. I am proud to have been and to still be a sex symbol. I am comfortable with my sexuality and cherish it. It is, after all, a gift.

I have often wondered why people did not understand or appreciate the work that people like myself do. I have often thought, "Why is what they do so much more sacred than what I do?" We are told as women who we should be at an early age in our culture and most people never question it.

People like myself have a gift of healing or at the very least creating a space where someone can choose to heal themselves. Our sexuality is a gift. It is a strong energetic presence inside each and every one of us as humans. It is as strong as our emotions, our mind, our physical being and our spirits. It is crucial that we humans are balanced and healed in these aspects for ourselves and for humanity. I have never been ashamed of what I have done or what I do. On the contrary, I am quite proud of it. I am who I am and I have lived a life that I have chosen for myself. How many others can say that?

Believe it or not the other most asked question that I get is "Have you ever had sex with John Holmes"? If you don't know and most people do, John Holmes was one of the most famous and prolific porn starts of all time. He once claimed to have had sex with 14,000 women, although that was thought to have been exaggerated. The answer is no, I did not have sex with John Holmes.

This was mostly because when I came into the business he was in the midst of a lot of problems. First he was in jail, and then he semi-retired and finally he was known for being HIV positive. This all went on just when I was getting into porn, so our paths did not cross much. I met him a few times at casting calls and once on a set, in San Francisco; the movie was called *Naughty Girls Like it Big*. It was starring Nina Hartley, Angel Kelly and myself. Angel Kelly was the one who was going to be working with John Holmes. I came back to the green room to relax and found John Holmes, laying on the couch sleeping. The PA, (Production Assistant) said to me that he was tired because he had just flown in, so

I sat quietly in a chair. John woke and sat up, looking sleepily at me. He asked who I was and I introduced myself. He then asked if I was the one he was going to be working with. I said no, the girl he was working with was my best friend and a beautiful woman. He smiled and that was the end of the conversation. I overheard a conversation between John and the PA, where John was lamenting about the fact that he had planted a bunch of rose bushes around his house, and the rose bushes were not blooming. They were healthy green plants but no sign of roses. This was very disturbing to John and he was sincerely asking for advice from the PA, about what to do to get his rose bushes to bloom. Word is that after John died, the rose bushes bloomed in many colors. Maybe things happen in time for a reason.

There is another question that cracks me up and I get it all the time. "Did you ever have an orgasm on camera?" Yes, yes and yes. I was usually able to orgasm easily on or off camera. I can't say that I did every single time, but when I couldn't get off it was usually due to extreme set conditions; for instance, making porn in the California desert with temperatures in the 100's, with sand blowing into every orifice, eating a cup of sand while giving a blowjob. Those are conditions that make it not so easy to get off. Sometimes it was just an uncomfortable position, like having sex in a kitchen sink or hanging from a pole. Sometimes it was just the end of a long day, call time at 7am and finally doing your double penetration scene at 2am; fuck, you have got to be kidding me! All I can say is, thank God I didn't have to get my cock hard.

I give the guys a ton of kudos for how they are able to perform physically on camera. Let's face it: a girl can always, lay back, breathe and fake a pretty good orgasm. I know some girls that do fetish work where they are paid to pretend to be unconscious when they get fucked. Talk about an easy job! But guys just do not have this luxury. They have got to get the cock hard and cum on cue. Now that's physical mastery. I always had a huge amount of empathy for all of my male co-stars. I would always check in with them before and during a sex scene to find out what they liked, what they needed to get hard, to stay hard and cum. Sometimes it was dirty talk that they liked; others wanted me to rub their nipples; there were some that could stay hard forever as long as I fingered their asshole. There was always some kind of trigger for all male porn stars.

I do not feel that male porn stars ever get their just due for their performances. The women get all of the glory, and sometimes higher wages, but the men do have longer staying power (no pun intended). The truth is that men in porn can stay gainfully employed into their 70's if they can still get it up and get it off, and believe me quite a few of them still can.

I have often been asked if I ever contracted an STD by working in porn. I might be one lucky soul, but in the 51 years I have spent on this planet doing the things that I have done, I pretty much got off without a scratch.

I have had gonorrhea once. I contracted it while at Michigan State, well before I ever acted in movies. There was a lot of partying going on there. We were voted the number one Party School by Time Magazine. We had the most outrageous Toga parties known to modern man. I still kind of miss those parties. That was back in the day when a toga party was considered wild. Nowadays I am sure most people have never even heard of them.

I contracted one STD while working directly in porn: I got chlamydia. It was on an all-girl set and a lot of girls got it. We figured that we passed it around in the girl-on-girl orgy, from the dildos and toys that we used to fuck every orifice of each other. But that was it. I thank my lucky stars, my guardians, Great Spirit and anyone else that in all of the years of engaging in truly, seriously wild sex, with completely unknown people all over the United States, Canada and Europe that I never contracted anything serious or life threatening. I honestly believe that I had good instincts that kept me safe, and if I didn't then I certainly had a guardian angel. I think it was a different world then, there was a time when the worst thing that I thought could happen was pregnancy, so I went on the pill; then the next thing was herpes, then there was HIV, so I never used needles or engaged in rough anal sex, or blood play, plus I would make sure I used condoms on everything and everyone. For all of the talk about contracting STD's it is odd how few people I knew in the business that came down with one of them.

12

One of the oddest experiences I had in my life full of odd experiences was when I went to work at the Bunny Ranch, which is owned by the infamous Dennis Hof, and was located in Carson City, Nevada. The Bunny Ranch, for those of you that don't know, is a legal brothel. I started working there very late in my career; about 1999, which made me 37 years old or so.

Dennis is an old friend of my mine and he had often suggested that I come to the Ranch. The Bunny Ranch opened up in 1955 and Dennis bought it in 1993. Dennis was actively bringing porn stars up to the Ranch as featured guests and had been doing so for a long time. At the time he was dating Sunset Thomas. Sunset was a well-known porn star who was said to have made a ton of money at the Ranch. According to some she was making $20,000 a night.

I had a sense of curiosity on how the Ranch was run as a business and I was looking forward to checking it out. The fact that it was a legal brothel intrigued me greatly. I wondered just how that worked in the United States, with the doctor check up to make sure you had no STD's, registration with the Sheriff as a legal prostitute, and so on. I kind of found it fascinating as a concept. I also wondered on how the day-to-day business went: how the clients picked the girls that they were going to have sex with and how much time was spent with each one. I even wondered who cleaned the rooms and sheets and stuff like that. I got an education while I was there, and it was certainly an interesting experience.

The thing that made me feel safe was that I had known Dennis for many years and had good faith that I was going to be well taken care of and all activities were going to be sane and consensual. I arrived at the Reno airport and true to Mr. Hof's style was picked up in a limousine. I was driven for many miles to Carson City where the Ranch was located.

All along the way I was seeing a bunch of brothels alongside the road; they were mostly made of trailers or small buildings. It was kind of funny to me because they appeared like 7-11 convenience stores along the road. I wondered to myself if there was really a market for this many brothels. Then I remembered who I was. Yeah, is there really a market for selling sex? Duh. The thing is there is always a market for any budget when it comes to selling sex. I always loved the George Carlin statement, "If selling is legal and sex is legal, than why the hell is selling sex not legal?" Good question. I never could come up with an answer for this. The hang-ups that people have around sex have never ceased to amaze me.

I arrived at the Ranch and to my surprise it was nothing but a bunch of trailers. They were *nice* trailers, mind you, but trailers just the same. They were hooked together, stabilized to the ground and nicely done… but a trailer is a trailer. I guess I was expecting some large castle-like building or something, although they do have a helicopter pad. You have to admit not every trailer park has a helicopter pad. The complex was surrounded by a chain link fence so it had a sense of security. Secured from what, I don't know, because it was literally in the middle of what I like to call Butt-Fuck Nowhere. Dennis, as well as a woman named Madam Suzette, who was the house mom at the Ranch, greeted me very warmly. The greeting room is very comfortable and welcoming, with a nice bar attached. I was shown to my room with its own bathroom, which was modestly decorated but nice.

I was then taken to the house doctor for a full examination and STD test. The house doctor was professional and completed his work swiftly. Fabulous job, no? He explained that my test results would be returned the next day in the morning at which point they would be sent to the Sheriff's office. The next day I went to the Sheriff's office, filled out my paper work to be a legal prostitute, paid my $275.00 fee and received my license to be a non-criminal cocksucker. I made a joke to my friends that I had a license to fuck. It had my picture on it and everything.

After all the preliminaries were completed, I began officially working on the floor. Luckily, I was assigned one of the regular girls, named Chloe, to assist me in navigating my way around, who I really needed. I still didn't really know how I went from meeting a client in the greeting room to getting him to pay me for a sexual act. Chloe explained that I would work a certain shift every day, say from noon to midnight and that anytime a customer entered the doors, a buzzer would go off in my room. That meant that I was suppose to report to the greeting room for what I call a Cattle Call, this is where all the girls who are on shift, line up, scant-ily dressed and get introduced to the customer. So imagine that you are a single male walking in a brothel, the minute you get through the door, about twenty scantily clad girls greet you, the Madam then asks you if you see something you like.

Now if it is a guy that comes all the time, he would usually just have a regular girl, but if not.... First of all if it's his first time, the poor customer is so intimidated by the experience he is shaking in his blue jeans, and of course he sees something he likes: he likes everything. He is so over-stim-ulated at this point that it's almost impossible for him to choose one. Cus-tomers like that would usually just go up the bar and order a drink. That's when the game was really on. Each girl had the ability to speak with, or better yet hustle the customer to get them to take a tour with them. This meant the guy would go to the girl's room where the girl would try to sell the customer on a certain sex act for a certain amount of time. For some reason this was called a party. I guess asking if you would like to party is nicer than asking if you would like to stick your cock up my ass. This hustling of customers was an art: sometimes they just picked the first girl that asked them to take a tour, and sometimes they sat at the bar for hours at a time, which never made the house really happy. Of course men being men, a lot just got off on the fact that there were twenty girls that "wanted" them. In reality the longer it took, the more pissed off most of us got.

Some of you may be surprised but I never made a good prostitute, hooker, or call girl; whatever you want to call it, I just wasn't good at it. I had a hard time hustling the guys at the bar and getting them to take a tour. I was used to guys chasing after me, not me chasing after them. It was hard for me to compete with the other girls for a guy's attention.

When I did manage to get them to take a tour, it was even more chal-lenging because I never knew how much to charge, for what specific sex act and then for how much time. I was completely out of my box of skill sets. Obviously a blowjob would be less than vaginal sex. What if the guy just wanted a hand job, was that less than a blowjob? What if you charged less but it took them twice as long to get off? I mean ,what if I say its one hundred bucks for a blowjob and the guy comes in ten seconds? I always felt sorry for guys, who claimed they didn't have that much money, so I would give them a deal and then later on I would see them pulling out their credit card to fuck another girl a little bit later.

I worked at the Bunny Ranch for about ten days straight and I could never get the right mindset. Yes, I did make a little money but not much for the amount of hours I spent on the floor. It always boggled my mind when a girl would claim that she had a $10,000 or $20,000 dollar party; remember there is a 50/50 split with the house plus your weekly expenses of food, room and board. All I can say is that I am glad I didn't have to rely on being a prostitute to feed myself because I probably would have starved to death long ago.

I was so bored there. My days were very routine, other than when I was on a shift. I would I wake up early in the morning and go off for my daily run. It seemed this was a completely foreign concept for the other girls at the Ranch. I couldn't stand being cooped up in that tiny building and never getting any fresh air, so my morning run was a godsend for me. I usually did a three to five mile run; there were lots of places to run since the Ranch is located in a pretty desolate place. You could probably run for about 20 miles without running into anyone else and anything else. The girls and the workers at the Ranch warned me to be safe while running. I reminded them that I was close to a black belt in martial arts; and besides, what was I supposed to be safe from? Was a rabbit, a coyote or maybe an alien from outer space going to abduct me?

All-in-all, the Bunny Ranch is a wonderful place to work. They take excellent care of everyone that works there. There is a great chef who prepares three wonderful meals a day, the whole place is extremely clean and the girls are very easy to get along with.

It's just too bad that I suck at being a prostitute.

13

Although I was first exposed to BDSM while working at Cinema X as a peep booth girl, the real catalyst for my late-life change happened when I chained Joey Silvera to a bidet in Hamburg and fucked his brains out. I loved that and it still gives me a tingle up my thighs thinking about it today. I love the thought of chaining a man up and fucking him, until he begs for mercy. I also enjoy being tied up and at the mercy of a play partner who turns me on. There is something about the complete dominance and consensual ownership of another person sexually that simply cannot be explained unless you have felt it yourself. And if you have felt it yourself then you probably want to feel more of it. I know that I did. I am also a very kinky fuck. I adore latex, leather, corsets, stockings, high heels and boots and I especially love to fuck in them. There is no larger sexual buzz kill, than to be all dressed up in latex with stockings, garters and screamingly tall heels and have the person that you are going to fuck ask you to take off your clothes.

The whole point of dressing up is to enjoy the look, the feel, the smell, and the touch of the clothes. Maybe it's just because of me being jaded by vanilla sex but I find men and women dressed in fetish clothes so much more arousing than if they were naked. This appreciation for the fetish clothes needs to be mutual as well. So if I am dressed up and the other person is "just not really in to it, this is a buzz kill as well. Luckily there are a lot of kinky people on the planet who also share many of my fetishes so it's not hard to find a good match. I have a ton of fetishes. I like to be tied up and teased to orgasm; I like to be gagged with a piece of cloth; I like to be spanked; I like to have my backside flogged with a thick leather flogger—no stingy whips, please; I love to have my feet massaged and my toes sucked; oh, yes, please talk dirty to me. I have lots of other fetishes that are not so obvious. I love Egyptian cotton sheets-they make me orgasm every time I get into bed; horseback riding (ok maybe this one is obvious); I love to be bathed in a large tub, where a man or woman puts me in bathtub filled with warm, fragrant water and washes me from head to toe. I especially love having my hair washed: I love the feel of someone who truly adores me running their hands through my hair washing me.

What makes a fetish, you ask? Well, the actual definition from Webster's goes something like this: Fetish—an object believed by certain primitive peoples to embody a spirit and exert magical powers; an idea, practice regarded with excessive or irrational reverence; the centering of strong sexual emotion in objects (e.g. shoes or furs)or parts of the body not normally associated with such emotion. Porsche's definition: Fetish—an object, idea, sensation that creates sexual arousal to the point of orgasm, or when combined with sexual stimulation creates a heightened state of orgasm. I truly believe that everyone has at least one fetish and most likely many more.

As my porn career was winding down, I looked at the possibility of doing other types of movies, still within the adult arena but different. I know that it is probably impossible to believe that I could be bored making fuck films. But yes, it happened to me. At a certain point, the sex becomes very mundane, rote, vanilla, one does the same positions over and over with a cum shot ending. Being a veteran on the set, the director would usually say to be "just give me a couple of good positions, some good, hard fucking, a little oral and a pop shot" The "pop shot" is the cum shot, most certainly, where the male porn star jerks his cock off to the point of exploding on the female porn star's tittles, ass, tummy or face. Because you as the viewer would most certainly not believe that the male porn star had really cum if you didn't see it. Sometimes the female porn star would attempt to catch the jizz on her tongue, swirling it around her mouth before swallowing it. "You get extra points if you can create stringies," said Jerrod Damino, who was the director of *Deep Throat*, when you do this oral cum shot. And yes, all of this can get very boring after eight years or so.

Everyone wants something different sexually deep down inside and with mainstream porn it was all just a lot of fucking. Sometimes the most sexual feeling occurs when there is no fucking at all.

As I mentioned before, I love sex and that is a big part of the reason I was successful and got work in the business, and inevitably it showed in my performances. I always made my scenes fun; I always got to know the person or people that I was going to be fucking on the set. We talked about what we did and didn't like sexually and so on. I was having a great sex life. I was now about 32 years old and the sex that I was having was simply the best. I was truly in my sexual prime. I was getting laid by some of the hottest guys and girls ever. But the sex that I was doing on film was really starting to bore me. I always wondered how I could bring the super hot sex that I was having off camera to the camera.

One of my dear friends suggested that I try making some BDSM movies. The only thing about that was that I would have to get training and would most likely has to start at the bottom and work my way to the top. There was no way that anybody was going to let me use a whip, until I had experienced it for myself. This was old school training but I got it and I understood why it was set up this way. It was really the only way to learn, by experiencing the ties that bind, the whip that stings and the snarl of a Mistress. I managed to get a lot of jobs working as a submissive while enjoying it as well.

I was in incredible shape because I was still dancing, so I made a great fetish model. I did look incredible tied up in rope, gagged and helpless. Great riggers such as Ernest Greene, Star Chandler, Alexis Payne, and Midori were all people that I had the pleasure of being tied up by. I adored being bound, I loved the intense attention I received while being tied, and I loved the feel of restraints against my skin and the helpless feeling. I have a big secret: I still love being bound to this day, especially by good lover. There is nothing like the feeling of being tied, gagged and helpless and having a dominant man look in my eyes with lust and passion, wanting me so bad his cock is about to explode. If one can do it, it stays with me for a long time.

Power exchange is all around us. It is a part of our lives from the moment that we are born until the moment we die. By agreeing to engage consciously in the many aspects of Dominance and Submission, we are given a training ground for all other forms of power exchange. It can be an incredible healing space for all 5 aspects of our humanness- emotional, mental, physical, spiritual and sexual. We will all face times of control and no control, of slavery and freedom, by our own choices, the force of another or nature. Our success will be measured by "how" we navigated the space. Were we able to simply surrender with receptivity, were we able to take leadership with active compassion, or did we choose to fight a no control battle with blame, resistance and doubt? This is the depth of what b/d/s/m has to offer an individual if they are willing to engage fully.

I loved being submissive, I loved surrendering control over to another. In the movies it was usually a very beautiful woman who would own me, and she would be wearing some really hot fetish clothing. I loved that fact that I wasn't in control, that I wasn't the one who had to think about what was going to happen in the scene. I loved the fact, that all I had to do was react to the Mistress's instructions, wants and desires. I would get on my knees and I would submit and do what she said. Anything she said it was my pleasure to serve.

It was the purest form of acting that is reacting to the stimulus of another person or persons. I couldn't deny the feelings and the sensations. I learned very quickly about turning the pain into pleasure. I learned very quickly that being in "sub space" was a beautiful thing. "Sub space" for me was a place of solitude, a place of letting go of thinking, a place that was my own personal utopia. I learned to trust only myself, to trust myself not to allow any harm or permanent damage to my flesh. I could take a very hard flogging, which was my favorite thing to have happen. I loved it all, whether it be spanking, paddling, nipple clamps, or a crop; I would say, "Yes, mistress," and I would obey.

I worked and played as a Submissive/Masochist for a couple for years. During the experience I was always stalking out the other side of the fence. I not-so-secretly still wanted to be a Dom. I loved being in control of things; is there anything more powerful than being in control of another person? Is there anything sexier than having someone completely at your mercy that trusts you to do what you will with him or her? I think not. I was ready to be the one that held the leash instead of the one that wore the collar.

I had several small attempts at being the Dom; this would happen at play parties and things of that nature. I was physically large at 5'10" and about 140 solid pounds of muscle, which produced a very domineering energy at play parties. Inevitably slaves would come up to me, they would start handing me whips to use on them, because I looked like a Dom. I wanted to do more than just look like a Dom. I wanted to be the real thing. I started studying the scene from a historical background. I read a lot about dominance and what it meant to be a true Dom. I read a lot by Eric Stanton and of course my absolute favorites were Irving Claw and Bunny Yeager, who produced the most famous Bettie Page. I adored Bettie Page; at the time I simply worshipped her. I spent a lot of time emulating her poses, her wardrobe and her wicked smile. There was something amazingly hot about looking at her all tied and trussed up and gagged with her amazing ass being spanked with a paddle and she never lost the pure joyful look on her face or in her eyes. She was one of the sexiest women of all times.

I learned everything that I could about all of the famous Doms in America and in Europe. I started getting magazines like Domination Directory International, Marquis and Skin Two. I went to every play party I could, did every movie that came my way, and I started to occasionally get small Domina roles. I immersed myself into the world of BDSM; it was a whole new world for me and my sexuality. I loved it. It stimulated me in every way emotionally, physically, mentally, spiritually and sexually.

I started getting into kinky sex; the kinkier it was, the better. I purchased closets full of fetish clothing. I loved really good fetish clothing: leather corsets, tall leather boots, long leather gloves, latex dresses and super high heels. I couldn't get enough and still can't. I love having sex in kinky fetish clothing. It is a total buzz kill if a guy asks me to remove my heels, take a latex cat suit off or a corset and stocking off before fucking him. Why would I want to take these totally hot clothes off for sex? I just don't get that. The idea is that they're totally hot clothes: just wearing them gets my pussy all wet, and hopefully your cock hard as you watch me in them and then we fuck.

I became a very good Domina in a short time. I started getting a lot more Dom parts offered to me in movies; it was now about 1993. I was pretty much working exclusively as a Dom in movies and started thinking about doing it for pay in real life as well. I had procured a job at Lady Laura's dungeon in Hollywood, which was one of the longest running dungeons in history. Laura was a great Domina and a truly wonderful Head Mistress. She is very respected in the industry and I learned a lot from her. At the time I was still traveling with my burlesque show although my trips were down to about ten to twelve a year instead of thirty. I eventually opened a small dungeon of my own in Los Angeles, which was very close to Venice Beach. Several famous Dominas rented out an apartment building with me to get this started. The building was small and held about six 2-bedroom units. We managed to rent out the entire unit, turning them all into little mini-dungeons. The theory was that by renting out the whole unit the neighbors would not complain and we would have the whole scene to ourselves. It was a good theory and it worked. We all had great dungeons; we all knew each other and had each other's backs. I worked as an independent Domina for several years, all the while honing my skills and challenging myself to find out what I enjoyed, and playing in my new playground. I really felt like that was the scene for me, a great big playground. I had lots of big equipment, like bondage tables and Saint Andrews Crosses, to small equipment like whips and restraints and tons of wardrobe costuming. As you all must know by now, I love costumes. What more could a girl ask for? I had the dungeon by Venice Beach for about three years.

In that time I had started traveling to Phoenix to study with a Medicine Man and Shaman. I had also met a woman in NYC named Tara Indiana who owned a dungeon there and proposed the idea of me being a traveling Dom, meaning that I would come to NYC to work as a Dom for a week, just like if I was a feature dancer in a club. It made perfect sense, a feature Mistress in a dungeon could do very well financially visiting three to four times a year. I took Tara up on her offer. It was called The Den of Iniquity.

As things progressed, I desired to leave Los Angeles. I wanted to move; I had just lived through the riots with Rodney King and then there was the bad earthquake in Northridge. LA had started to eat my soul, or maybe more accurately I had allowed LA to eat my soul; maybe I had even fed the city my soul. Regardless of how it happened, my soul was dangerously close to being consumed and I needed to get out. I felt like I was being choked. I had developed the most horrendous anxiety attacks. I started to look for other cities to live in. I had the real desire to live in an entirely different city or even another state. I looked at San Francisco, San Diego and Las Vegas; all of these places were fairly expensive and I didn't have much money saved up for a big move. Since I was driving back and forth to Phoenix almost every month, I looked at rental prices and found it was something that I could afford. I liked Phoenix; it was fresh, new. I could breathe, the anxiety attacks decreased when I was there and my teachers were there as well. I decided to move to Phoenix.

This time I moved with minimal things. Basically I left with just the clothes on my back, I either sold or gave away almost everything that I owned. I never understand why people are so attached to things. I moved with a very small U-Haul truck, with my clothes, some music and a couple of suitcases. I rented a large three-bedroom apartment with a friend. We each had a bedroom and we turned the spare bedroom into a working room. We both traveled a lot, so we were rarely there but when we were, we both had clients that we were able to see in the spare room. My roommate's clients were getting massages, and mine were practicing BDSM.. I eventually moved out of the apartment to a three-bedroom house of my own. I turned the master bedroom into a dungeon. By this time I had gotten pretty good at turning spare bedrooms into dungeons. This house was small in a quiet neighborhood and I could go on undetected for as long as I liked. The year was 1999. I was still working in NYC with Tara Indiana; in fact I was spending a lot more time in NYC than ever. My relationship with Tara was always a bit precarious, but I loved NYC and I always enjoyed being there.

I had several lovers both male and female, who were my playmates of BDSM. I was able to still go out to the clubs in NYC, like HellFire, the Vault, Paddles, La Trapeze. I really had everything that a girl could want. My life was good. Things stayed this way until 2003, when I opened the dungeon in Phoenix. Tara and I had several confrontations that were unresolved. It seemed the best thing for me to do was to part ways with her. She is a good woman and I wish her well but it was time to more forward.

This meant that I was probably not going to be visiting NYC for a while, so I would need to find or create a way for me to make a living in Phoenix. I knew the market was strong in Phoenix for a dungeon. The market was not over saturated; it was big enough to support the lifestyle but small enough so that there wasn't one on every corner already. There were always plenty of kinky people who wanted sessions. If people want something, and people always do, there will always be supply and the demand.

When one has a kink or a fetish, often people in their lives don't understand it or they look down on it and project judgments. The guy who wants to be dressed in women's clothing and fucked in the ass, or the guy who wants to be trained like a dog is forced into silence. They don't want their bosses to know that they are wearing a bra & panties under their business suit; they can't tell their buddy at the bar that what they really want is to be handcuffed to the bar rail and have the bartender pull down their pants and spank them so hard they can't sit down comfortably for the rest of the night. It really is hard to be a person with a different sexual template and often people that do are made out to be freaks, perverts or worst-case scenario, mentally ill, psychopathic and sociopathic.

Submissive men are in the same place quite often. They might be married but their wife isn't going to tie them up and slap their face. If they go out on a date they are not going to ask the woman if it is okay if they grovel on the floor and lick her boots. They ask me to do the things that the women in their world would never do or they are simply to frightened to ask for. They ask me to give action to the thoughts that stimulate their minds. I breathe the breath of life into their imaginative fantasies; always safe, sane and consensually.

Often people wanted sessions with someone other than myself. I was often asked for a Dom with big boobs, or maybe with dark skin, or a more petite body. So I knew that the possibility of other Doms getting sessions under my roof was strong as well. I was fairly certain that the market in Phoenix would support a dungeon. The legalities seem to be about the same as everywhere. Adult businesses need to stay within a proper zone in Phoenix, which meant if I was going to have a legal building it would be located somewhere in the warehouse district in the city of Phoenix and provide absolutely no sexual services. I hired a lawyer to do the research for me on opening a dungeon. I started to look for a building; this was the hardest thing at first. I hired real estate people, talked with lots of agencies about what I was looking for. There were a lot of small places 500-800 square feet or large places like 10,000-20,000 square feet. I needed a building about 5,000 square feet. The last building that we had in NYC was about six to seven thousand square feet. I needed something big enough to house three-to-five session rooms with a couple of offices and such. After many weeks of frustration at not being able to find a building, I picked up the Sunday paper and decided to go old school at finding a place. Yes, I was going to look through the Sunday paper to find a building.

It worked. I found a 5,000 square foot building in the warehouse district for a great rent price. I arranged to look at the building and it was everything that I could possibly want. It was freestanding with a fence-secured parking lot, it was easily accessible from four major freeways, it was close to the airport and had a great price I rented the building that very day and moved in quickly. My main mission was to get at least one room ready to session in as soon as possible.

That meant it needed paint and new carpet, which had to be fitted quickly, and phones and a bunch of other shit. I had three rooms usable in about a week. I had the pleasure of having a couple of girls already working with me as staff. We managed to answer the phone, do sessions, get the bills paid and have a little fun as well. I needed to arrange a different name for my dungeon, since Tara Indiana held the trademark on the Den of Iniquity. I had already started a lot of business matters in the acronym DOIAZ. I was now challenged with how was I going to change that into a new name. I researched a lot of Latin names, looking for something that would fit DOI, the AZ piece was easy because of Arizona of course. I came up with Den of Indomitus, meaning of Cave of the Indomitable/Unconquerable/Untamed. I liked this and it would easily fit with DOIAZ, which meant that I wouldn't have to change a bunch of paper work.

I would like to say that in the time I have been working in this area, I have seen or heard it all. Every time I say or think this is true, someone walks through the door just a little kinkier than anyone I have ever seen. Which is fine of course. For the most part, yes, I have seen and heard it all. I once had a saying that no session was too kinky or taboo for me. I wanted clients to feel like they were safe to express those locked-up fantasies. The saddest thing is that usually what they have to express is not that bad or taboo. It is usually something like "I like to dress in my wife's panties and fuck myself with a dildo. But I would really like it if you would force me into a pair of satin panties and fuck me with your strap-on cock." "I want to drink your piss from a champagne glass." "I want to be forced to lick your boots and whipped into submission." "I want to be forced into diapers and treated like a baby." These are all things that are part of someone's sexual template and are nothing to be ashamed of at all. What turns you on turns you on, as long as you act on it safely with consent from all involved.

These requests by men all sound fairly normal to me and to most Dominas the world over. The one thing that I can say for certain is that there is never a dull day in the dungeon. I still run a very old school dungeon meaning that it is female owned and operated and there are no sexual services provided of any kind. I know this is going to be hard to believe but it really is true.

To a lot of true kinksters, sex is just an afterthought. It isn't about intercourse, it is about living out a fantasy that involves power exchange and kink. Plus, the reality is that providing any type of sexual service would be unlawful in most places in the United States. While most men are sincerely looking to fulfill long-time expressions of their sexuality, for the most part they are not looking to cheat on their beloved or commit adultery.

After being inducted into the Hustler Hall of Fame, I was invited to have dinner with Larry Flynt and many others joined us. At dinner Mr. Flynt made a comment about me owning a dungeon and something to the fact that he didn't understand why someone would want to get their ass beat without getting fucked. I laughed and said that I understood why he thought that.. I also said that I didn't understand his obsession with putting girls in porno movies the day after they turned 18 years old but I would still defend his right to do so. He laughed.

There is never a session that is just like another session. They are all extremely different, even if it's just the person. I have managed to have days were it seemed that everyone has the same theme. "I want to be dominated, bound, spanked, flogged; I want some cock & ball torture and to be fucked in the ass." I have had days were I have heard the same things requested by six different guys, in the same day, which always makes me wonder if there is something up with the planetary alignment. Every once in a while, someone requests something and even I have to stop for a moment, "You want me to what?" Those requests sound something like this: "I want you to dress up in a Mommy dress, and step on small furry plushy animals, while you scream at me, telling me what a bad boy I am, and how you are going to put me over your knee, pull my pants down and spank my bare ass." "I want you to dress up like Catwoman; I am going to be Wonder Woman and we are going to have a cat fight!" "I am a Jewish Sissy Slut and you are my Nazi Captor." "I want you to hunt me with an air-soft pistol." "I want you to force me to eat a large box of Chinese food, one can of tuna, one can of ravioli, and two cans of corn. Then I want you to put six cleansing suppositories into my rectum with a two-quart soapy enema. While I hold the enema, I want you to force me to vomit all the food at which point I will then be allowed to expel the enema"

The reality is that none of these activities are that extreme or repulsive. Of course some things that I do turn me on more than others, but I always feel that I give every client my best at what he wants to explore.

I love what I do. I honestly enjoy driving to work each day. I am going to a building that I built and decorated; it is like going to my own private tree house or hideaway. The building kind of looks like a fortress on the outside, with the decorative razor wire around the top of the fencing in the back parking lot. When I was little, I could never really figure out what I wanted to be when I grew up. I could never really decide. I liked the idea of being a Doctor, I loved the idea of being a Police Officer, and I adored the idea of being a Cowboy. In the end, I always thought, that I wanted a job where I could go every day and be happy. Something I really liked doing because then it wouldn't be work, it would be fun. I would never have the need to retire. Well, that's pretty much what I have at this point.

Okay, yes, there are times when I dread going to work; there are days or nights when I would rather be getting a root canal. Yes, it does happen. Being a Head Mistress is a lot like running any small business. I guess most of the job is very dull, boring, mundane, and oh, did I mention that it is not glamorous at all? The not glamorous stuff: things like vacuuming, mopping floors, changing air filters, light bulbs, picking up trash in the parking lot and let's not forget that at times the only thing that I am mistress of is the laundry. So much of it is dull and boring and mundane. Sometimes I need to go shopping for supplies; I call this my Costco run, and all of the above can also go into this category. I need to place advertising and to make sure the website is up to date. I have to pay utility bills. I tell my staff that I am the one who keeps the magic in the box, meaning the electric box; some of my staff seems to think it's true and that power is free and endless. Not quite. Some of my other duties include things like maintaining equipment, organizing schedules, interviewing and hiring and so on.

Come to think of it, the only glamorous Head Mistress duties that I have are when I attend a convention or an event. I get dressed up, look fabulous, get lots of photos taken of me, and talk to people: that's glamour. But those moments are few and far between. I still do sessions because I really do enjoy them. I love the one-on-one connection with the people. I love getting into their heads so to speak.

As I write this, I am currently fifty-one years old; to me that sounds pretty old. I remember meeting Maitresse Francois, a wonderfully beautiful Domina in Paris, France, many years ago; at the time I was thirty years old and she was fifty or so. She had a dungeon in the heart of Paris and was still doing sessions. I thought that was pretty amazing, the fact that she was still working and doing what she loved at fifty years old when everything else that I had experienced in the adult business would have kicked me to the curb at thirty. This was before the fabulous MILF sensation.

Things will happen in the dungeon that are really quite funny. There was one guy that we used to call Smokin' Tom. He was a guy who would fly into Phoenix for what he called smoking sessions, especially cigar smoking sessions. Tom loved to have cigar smoke blown into his face. He would request that the Mistress sit very close to him while smoking a cigar and literally blow the smoke right up his nose. He would plug one of nostrils with toilet paper, he got into restricting his breathing. I would try to time the exhale of the cigar smoke at the same moment that he would have to inhale. He also loved to have one of his eye lids forced open and the cigar smoke blown directly into his eye.

Tom's sessions would last anywhere from three to five hours, for two to three days and involve two to four different Mistresses. He would session in one of my smaller session rooms, the room would be completely filled with smoke. The Doms would smoke about twelve to twenty large cigars in the course of his session. He would often insert a cigar into his ass to receive more nicotine. After one particularly grueling session Jim was unable to remove the cigar from his ass, apparently it had slid up so far that he could not retrieve it. He worried that it wouldn't come out and that he might have to visit a doctor to have it removed. I suggested that he go back to the hotel, relax, and take a hot bath and that the cigar would eventually come out. He called me a few hours later to let me know that the cigar had indeed come out. He was quite relieved! The other interesting thing about Jim was that he was a very religious man. He loved Jesus and started every session by discussing Jesus and reading some excerpts from the Daily Bread. There's nothing like reading about Jesus before you watch a guy shove a cigar up his ass.

There was a guy that we called Old Man David; he was a regular client who visited the Den every week or so. He was a kinky old man who loved to be dominated and bound; he loved having his cock and balls tortured, he loved to be pissed on and sometimes he even liked to be shit on. This is always interesting, having to shit sometime during your session. I had a visiting Mistress from NYC, who was new to the Den; she was young and beautiful, named Madison. Apparently David had taken his false teeth out before or during the session, wrapping them in a paper towel and sitting them on the table. As Madison cleaned up during the session, she had unwittingly thrown the paper towel-wrapped teeth in the garbage. When the session was over, David could not find his teeth. Madison came to the office asking if anyone had seen her client's teeth. We all looked somewhat shocked and perplexed. It took several of us going through several large bags of trash to find the teeth, amongst a lot of laughter and joking around. We did eventually find old man David's teeth. Such a glamorous life I lead as a professional Dom, right?

Christmas 2000, I love this holiday.

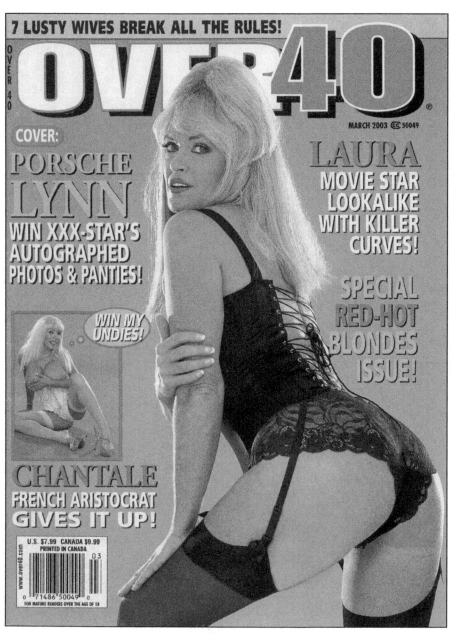

Last Magazine Cover, for the lovely Diane Hansen.

Me in my real Martial Arts gyi, sexy style.

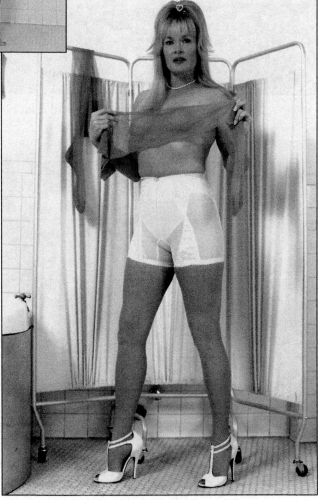

Venus Delight, Robin Byrd & me.

Latex dress by Polymorph, love
them, 2000.

Behind the camrea, for real, Berlin, 2001.

With Bill Margold, Free
Speech Coalition, 2002.

AVN Convention,
Vegas, 2005.

Legends of Erotica at The Whiskey on Sunset Strip.

Halloween, DOIAZ, 2004.

With Tara Indiana at the DOINYC booth, 2001.

In my prime,
DOINYC, 2002.

DomCon LA, 2006.

Head Mistress, DOIAZ, 2010.

Standing on top of a man.

With Midori, Bond Con Vegas.

Stacey Burke at BondCon NYC.

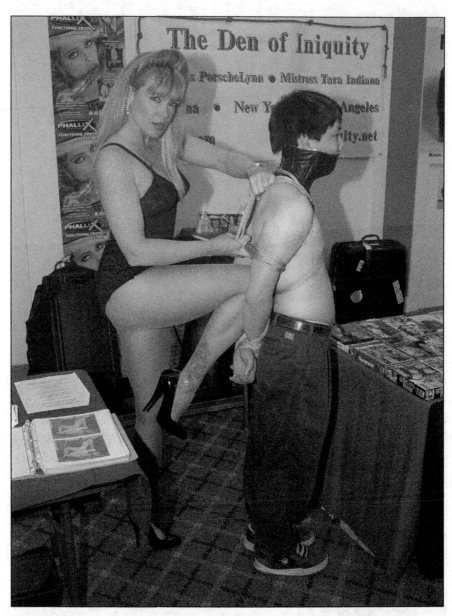

The joy of restraing another, BondCon, NYC.

Tied Up, at DomCon LA, 2009.

Spanking Playboy girl Julie Meadows.

Latex catsuit by House of Harlot, Firearm American Arms.

Head Mistress, DOIAZ, 2010.

Fetish Prom, Phoenix, AZ, 2013

Smothering Ron Jeremy with Selena Steel.

In front of Stonghenge.

Shooting Autral-Asian Championship.

14

So many people think that porn stars lead the life of the damned when they leave the business. Nothing could be further from the truth. Although some people that worked in adult films go on to leave troubled lives, this is true of any profession. I have moved on and continued to be a woman who values individuality, autonomy, life, liberty and the pursuit of happiness.

My home is still located in Phoenix, Arizona. I love the state and the state of mind that it creates.

I would say that while my life is a paradox, it is a paradox of all of the things that make it worth living. I have a life that is full of many things that are somewhat contradictory. I do not see this as much of a problem as others do. I never quite understood why we all have to fall under the same belief systems. Basically my philosophy is this: I have given up looking for the meaning of life and have decided to live a life with meaning. No, I did not come up with this saying. I borrowed it, but still I think it fits me quite well.

I still own and operate the Den of Indomitus, which is Arizona's only fully equipped dungeon. I still do sessions. I do these for a few reasons. First and foremost, I do them because I truly enjoy the one-on-one personal experience that happens while sessions occur, and while there is no sex in the sessions, it is still the most intimate sexual space that I have ever experienced. I love that there is never any one day that is exactly like the next. God knows that my spirit would be completely broken working in a 9-to-5 job, doing the same thing day after day.

Speaking of God and Spirit, I am an apprentice on a shamanic path and have completed 18 Sundances. Most people will ask what the hell does that mean or what the hell is a shamanic path? Well, I will tell you. A shamanic path is most often rooted in one of the Mystery Schools of the Eight Great Powers. Now that I have you even more confused, let's break down the word shamanic path. Shamanism is the ability to align (which is the opposite of repulsion) with the elements, which are water, earth, wind, fire and the void. It involves the ability to align with the worlds of Grandmother Earth, which are the plant world, the mineral world, animal world, human world and the spirit world. It focuses on the ability to travel from the tonal to the naqual, from substance to spirit, from the 3rd dimension to the 5th dimension and so forth. This might sound wild to the uninitiated but there are a lot of simple steps and exercises along the way to get one to the point where they want to be.

Shamanism has existed on the planet for all time and since all time, all over the planet. As an ex-communicated Catholic, I never really understood the Christian religion. While I have deep respect for those who follow it, I never really understood it. I understand that people need a place to be with their community and feel whole; I do not judge. With that said the whole hell and damnation thing, the whole Jesus died for our sins; Jesus will save us and all that. I just don't buy it. First of all, if there really is a hell it must be a resting place for those individuals that choose Hate and Wrath over Love and Beauty. I also have another saying that I have lived by: a religion is for people who are afraid to go to hell and a spiritual path is for people who have already been there. I have seen much hate, wrath and pure evil, and somewhere along the way I did not choose to follow. I chose instead to follow a way of love, beauty, being benevolent and compassionate. I chose to heal my needy, wounded, abandoned little girl, heal my revengeful, manipulative adult and step onto a path with power, my path with heart. This is what my shamanic path is to me. I don't expect people to understand nor do I seek their approval.

It's the nice thing about being 51 years old: I don't really care what people think any more. I did at one time; many of my actions were based on getting approval from others, wanting to be loved or liked. I don't know if it's just the old age thing or the fact that I have sundanced in the high desert, in the heat of the summer, for 3 days and 3 nights without food and water. While I am there I am seeking a vision from spirit, seeking to better myself, and to purify my mind, body and soul. I know that it has worked and that I am certainly a better person than I have ever been. I have elemental balance and I am truly able to give to myself my life and others with beauty, for me that am the best I can be. I often think, when I am dying or dead what do I want to have accomplished from this lifetime? I desire to have gained knowledge and known great pleasure. That is my meaning and purpose to life. Life does not give you a meaning and purpose; you must give your life meaning and purpose. It took me many years to get to this place. I can honestly say that I am most content where I am. I truly have a wonderful life. I have always had a wonderful life even when it wasn't so pretty; I just wasn't awake enough to realize it. My spiritual path isn't something that I do once a week like most churches ask you to do. My spiritual path is a way of life. I walk my path every day in every way.

Another thing that I truly enjoy at this point in my life is shooting. I am an avid shooter. I am an NRA instructor as a Distinguished Expert in Pistols and Rifles. I am a competitive sport shooter and a hobbyist. I enjoy shooting pistols or handguns mostly, but I also enjoy shooting rifles and shotguns. My favorite pistol is a CZ75 with a fiber optic front site and purple Hello Kitty grips! My shotgun is a Remington 800 with a Fobar front lite mount, ghost ring site, side saddle and a Raven engraved on the side because it was customized at the renowned Gunsite Academy, where I have taken both the pistol & shotgun class. Living in Arizona gives me the ability to shoot year 'round. I shoot with several local clubs. I shoot Steel Challenge, United States Practical Pistol and IPSC-International Pistol Shooting Competition. I won the Ladies Stock Auto World Hand gunner Championship in 1999 and have won many other titles as well.

I used to be terrified of guns. I first learned to shoot to get over my fear of guns that had ruled my life up to this point. As I mentioned briefly before, my Father had shot my Mother in front of my Grandmother and me. My Father later shot himself. This incident created a huge armor on me in many ways, as you can only imagine. I created many stories and myths to try to cope with what had happened. Many of those stories revolved around guns. I thought, "Guns are bad; guns kill people; if only we could get rid of all of the guns, nobody would die". It was much easier to blame things on guns than face what had really happened.

I lived by these stories for many years but at the same time I became obsessed with other people's stories, especially other people who had gone through what I had gone through or even people who had gone through worse things than I had. If misery loves company, pity loves knowing that someone has had a worse time. As I got older, I realized that I had created a huge fear inside of myself, and that fear had a sizable amount of control over me. Being a Super Control Freak, I hated this. I was on a mission to remove any fears that I had. I started with little things first, and worked my way further along, towards the bigger things that ruled my mind.

I was in fear of being in a committed relationship; I conquered that. I was afraid of the dark, I had a fear of confined spaces; when I beat those I moved on to more. These seemed like bigger things: fear of heights, fear of scuba diving (which I am not completely over yet), and of course, fear of guns. My plan of attack was to do everything that I was afraid of, in a good way. So, I went to a shooting range to get lessons on shooting and firearms. I found the whole topic fascinating: how the guns work, how the ammo works, and so on. I remember when I started my first shooting lesson, I had previously warned the instructor that I was incredibly afraid of guns. As I stood on the firing line, sweating, shaking, eyes tearing up, the instructor walked me through firing my first shots.

At first each time the gun went off, the sound triggered a flashback to the dreaded day that my Grandmother & I had witnessed my father shooting my mother. As I shot more, I realized what I really needed to heal was myself and to stop blaming the guns for what had happened. I realized the only thing that I was in control of was my thoughts, my mind. I realized that I needed to accept what had happened without pity and loathing. I needed to forgive my Father and myself for all the hatred, wrath that I had been carrying around inside of me. This didn't happen overnight, it took many years of diligent, ceremonial work on my part and a lot of patience on my teacher's part to be where I am today. With that said, I can truly say that I have healed from what happened and have found peace and forgiveness.

I love to shoot and truly enjoy teaching people to shoot. I stand on a firm knowing that each of us have the right as human beings as well as the Constitutional Right to defend our lives and the lives of others against clear and imminent danger. That each and every one of us has the right to keep and bear arms and that it shall not be infringed on. I know that the gun is not the Devil; the gun is an innocent tool. The Devil is the person who chooses to do evil things with the gun. With a quick history recapitulation we can clearly see that when there were no guns, humans found other ways to kill each other. The only way this is going to be "fixed" is by fixing the "heart" of mankind. It's not going to be fixed by destroying the tool. The evil inside of mankind that turns them into a killer must be destroyed.

I now have a fairly simple, drama-free, humble life. I mix my work schedule with fun and things that give me pleasure as well as what I call tithing, giving it back or paying it forward. I completely believe that each of us has the duty to give back to life and others acknowledging the gifts that we have received. I do this in several ways, volunteering to do many things on my shamanic path. I am on a crew that takes "care" of our beloved Ceremonial Land. This means everything from maintenance on structures, such as installing insulation and windows, or maintenance of landscape, which means doing things such as mowing lawns, fertilizing trees, digging ditches, creating walkways, etc. I am a Purification lodge Fire Chief, which means that I am in charge of preparing the fire for the purification lodge. I am also a Sacred Pipe Carrier, Healing Dance Chief, and the North Keeper of the Purification lodge.

What I can say about where I am now is that, at 51 years old, I have healed my needy, wounded abandoned child as well as my revengeful, manipulative adult. I am grateful for my whole life, every minute of it. I have absolutely no regrets, but I do have remorse for the mistakes that I made along the way that caused others pain. When I was 20 or so, I thought that 51 was disgustingly old. I thought that I would most certainly be dead by then, so on some level it surprises me that I am where I am at this point in my life. It's the life that I always wanted, it's the life that I always dreamed was possible and to my credit, it's the life that I made.

It's the house that Porsche built.

Afterword

There comes a time in the course of one's life when one is invited to look back at their lives. If we are smart we look back before the memories have faded and thank those who stood beside us, gave us a push upwards or a smile. If we are wise, we look at our entire life, the good, the bad and the ugly. We take note of our mistakes, ask for forgiveness and grow. While I didn't appreciate the bad and the ugly when it was happening, I am grateful for the challenges that I faced and how I navigated them. Looking back at my 10 years in burlesque, porn and kink has been a wonderful, rich walk down memory lane. I am grateful for a life so abundant with beauty, power, challenge and many sweet memories. I would like to thank all of the women that have gone before me. They truly paved the way for me to freely express myself with passion, lust, liberty, and freedom.

I would like to thank all of the individuals that were instrumental in the creation of Porsche Lynn. A special mention goes out to Harry Mahoney, Mike Jolly, Reuben Sturman, Larry Flynt, Dino Ferrari, Lenny Bertram, Bill Margold, Bruce Seven, John Stagliano, Cal Vista, Brad Willis, Suze Randall, Andrew Blake, Alexis Vogel, Jim Bridges, Henri Pachard, Ron Sullivan, Fred Lincoln, David Jackson, Tara Indiana, Club Doma, HOM/London Video, BonVue, Ernest Greene, and Nina Hartley. I also want to thank every cameraman, photographer, director, producer, makeup artist, boom, lighting guy, DJ, roadie and faithful submissive or slave who ever served me, all the incredible women who, I have had the pleasure of knowing in the many dungeons around the world. I also thank Tony Sacre for his help in editing this book.

I give many thanks to all of the wonderful people that I have met along the journey of my life. Thank you for your love, support, generosity and patience. Much gratitude to my mother and father for giving life to me. I would like to give special thanks to Sweet Medicine Sundance Path, and to my beloved Naqual Thunderstrikes. Words cannot express my gratitude for being present with you on this journey called life.

Thank you to Brian Whitney for your support in writing this book, your encouragement to be true to myself, and for keeping me on deadline.

Made in the USA
Columbia, SC
06 June 2018